# Sought by
# GRACE

# Sought by
# GRACE

# Sought by
# GRACE

R. Kent Hughes

**MOODY PRESS**
CHICAGO

ISBN: 0-8024-1431-1


1 3 5 7 9 10 8 6 4 2

*Printed in the United States of America*

# CONTENTS

| | | |
|---|---|---|
| | Introduction | 9 |
| 1. | The Little Big Man | 11 |
| 2. | Your Heart's Ears | 25 |
| 3. | Narrow Is Wide | 43 |
| 4. | From Death Valley | 57 |
| 5. | Grace Through Faith | 71 |
| 6. | Not Far from the Kingdom | 85 |
| | Conclusion | 99 |

# INTRODUCTION

I was a high school student when I received the gift of God's saving grace. As I stared transfixed at Romans 10:9 and slowly read it out loud—"That if you confess with your mouth, 'Jesus is Lord,' and believe in your heart that God raised him from the dead, you will be saved"—I believed! It was as if the very words of that verse rose from the text, and came through my eyes and into my heart. That night, and the weeks that followed, I could not get enough of God's Word. The next day, I actually found the sky to be bluer and the grass greener. And I have continued to confess Jesus before anyone who will listen.

A friend soon introduced me to the helpful acrostic G–R–A–C–E, God's Riches At Christ's Expense, and it did me much good as those five letters kept before me the truth that grace is a gift from God, centered and mediated through His Son Christ Jesus.

Through the years I've learned that grace is a lavish, joyous word which describes God's perpetual inclination to bless His people. If grace could be contained in a water pitcher, then the pitcher would always be tilted to pour out a flood of grace. We were sought by grace, sustained by grace, and

*Grace has brought us safe*
*Thus far*
*And grace will*
*Lead us home.*

God's grace in bringing the Gospel to us defies any single description. The whole of God's Word informs it, especially the Gospels and Epistles. The best way to understand grace is through reading and rereading key texts. And that is what *Sought by Grace* is about. Its six chapters discuss in their order God's gracious seeking, the grace of hearing the Word, grace in the Gospel's narrowness, grace for dead people, grace through faith, and the kingdom of grace.

My experience is that many people in good churches do not fully grasp God's saving grace. So often when asked how they know that they are Christians they answer, "Because I accepted" or "I prayed" or "I went forward." Notice the prominence of *"I"*—which places the emphasis on what they have done. Rather the grace-emphasis must center on God alone—"Because Christ . . ." Grace begins with God and has its end in God.

So my prayer is that this little book will clear away the spiritual fog so that those who are uncertain of salvation can settle it once for all and know the riches of His grace:

*For you know the grace of our Lord Jesus Christ,*
*that though he was rich, yet for your sakes he*
*became poor, so that you through his poverty*
*might become rich.*
*(2 Corinthians 8:9)*

# *the little*
# BIG MAN

Charles Spurgeon, the famed Victorian-era preacher who preached to a congregation of five thousand both morning and evening, also established a Pastor's College, which exists to this day. A famous feature of the college experience was "the question oak," a large tree on Spurgeon's estate where, in good weather, students would gather on Friday afternoons to ask questions of Mr. Spurgeon and then deliver extemporaneous sermons. On one memorable occasion, Spurgeon called on a student to give a message on Zacchaeus. The student rose and said: "Zacchaeus was of little stature, so am I. Zacchaeus was up a tree, so am I. Zacchaeus came down, so will I."[1]

Zacchaeus's escapade makes for a fun story. The idea of a wee man perched like a bird in a tree (and found out!) is the stuff of humor and children's songs.

> *Zacchaeus was a wee little man*
> *and a wee little man was he.*
> *He climbed way up in a Sycamore tree,*
> *for the Lord he wanted to see. . . .*

This is a cute ditty for young children to recite, but the story occupies a very serious place in Luke's account of Jesus' life, because it is Jesus' last personal encounter before His arrival in Jerusalem and the events leading to His death. Significantly, the final line in the Zacchaeus story contains the summary line of the purpose of Jesus' ministry, "For the Son of Man came to seek and to save what was lost" (19:10). Saving the lost is what Jesus is about.

In this respect, the salvation of Zacchaeus has telling spiritual connections to the two events that precede it. Its connection to the healing of the blind beggar is obvious because the deliverance there of a man lost in blindness and poverty corresponds to the deliverance of a man lost in wealth and corruption.[2] And its connection to the story before that, of the Rich Ruler, is also very clear because what is stated there is humanly impossible, namely, the salvation of a rich man ("Indeed, it is easier for a camel to go through the eye of a needle than for a rich man to enter the kingdom of God," 18:25). This impossibility now takes place in the salvation of rich little Zacchaeus. In fact, the account of Zacchaeus is an account of how the impossible takes place—grace.

## DIVINE INITIATIVE

If I were in charge of casting for *Zacchaeus, the Movie* in the 1940s, I would have chosen diminutive Edward G. Robinson, who played Al Capone. Today, I would choose Danny DeVito as "Big Z." Those shifty eyes, his swagger—the perfect little big man.

From a tax-collecting perspective, Zacchaeus had it made. Taxes were collected at three places inland: Capernaum, Jericho, and Jerusalem.[3] Jericho, Zacchaeus's home turf, had a commanding position at the crossing of the Jordan River, one of the prime approaches to

Jerusalem. And Jericho was rich due to its great palm forests and balsam groves. As chief tax collector, he was head of a tax-farming corporation with collectors who extorted the people, and then paid him before he paid the Romans. "Big Z" was the kingpin of the Jericho tax cartel, and matched it with the scruples of a modern day crack dealer. Bottom line: he was wealthy, "filthy rich" in the fullest sense of the term. Not a likely candidate for God's kingdom!

Naturally, he was hated. In the eyes of his country-men, his littleness was more than physical. Some of the locals would have liked to put him through the eye of a needle—"squeezed out," as C. S. Lewis put it, "in one long bloody thread from tail to snout."[4]

No one would ever have guessed on that spring day that Zacchaeus would have wanted to see Jesus. But he did. As Luke says, "He wanted to see who Jesus was" (19:3a). Why? We wonder. Perhaps he had heard of the conversion of Levi (Matthew) the tax collector, who was now one of Jesus' followers (cf. 5:27–32). Perhaps he had even known Levi. Palestine was a small place, and tax collectors frequently hung out together. Because Jesus had ministered to Levi and others of his crowd, he had irked the religious establishment and was known as a friend of "tax collectors and sinners." Jesus evidently had a soft spot for people like Zacchaeus.

It is also very likely that Zacchaeus had found his wealth and lifestyle unsatisfying. No doubt, a sense of dis-ease had invaded his pleasures. Nothing seemed to be ful-filling, despite all his wealth and authority. The brief delights he experienced didn't last long. This lack of satis-faction is what drew Saint Augustine to Christ, as he wrote in retrospect to God: "Your goad was thrusting at my heart, giving me no peace until the eye of my soul could discern you without mistake" (Bk. VII, 8).[5] Like Augustine, Zaccha-eus was drawn by the severe mercy of dissatisfaction.

Also, it is very probable that Zacchaeus was weary of being hated by his people. When people hassled him he gave "as good as he got," but it was still a miserable way to be and feel. The relentless contempt of his people left him desolate and alone.

Thus, the restless little man determined to see Jesus, "but [alas!] being a short man he could not, because of the crowd" (19:3b). What pleasure this must have given the crowd—closing ranks so that the diminutive, hated tax collector couldn't see. What joy there would be in bumping the little man back, boxing him out. "Oh, sorry about the elbow, Zacchaeus, you're hard to see. Oh, that's your foot?"

Short or not, Zacchaeus had legs, and he used them—"So he ran ahead and climbed a sycamore-fig tree to see him, since Jesus was coming that way" (19:4). To be specific, it was a ficus sycomorus, a sturdy tree, some forty feet high, with a short trunk and wide branches, very easy to climb.[6] The picture of this tiny rejected man sitting alone, hidden in order to get a glimpse of Jesus, is very touching. He certainly didn't want the crowd to know he was there. He would get a private view. The crowd would pass. He would remain unseen, hoping for some unknown relief to the torment of his soul, but without making a personal connection to Jesus.

But the interior-driven initiative of Zacchaeus was matched by the exterior-graced initiative of Christ. "When Jesus reached the spot, he looked up and said to him, 'Zacchaeus, come down immediately. I must stay at your house today.' So he came down at once and welcomed him gladly" (19:5–6). As the song goes:

> *And as the Savior passed his way,*
> *he looked up in the tree.*
> *And he said, "Zacchaeus, you come down!*

*for I'm going to your house today,*
*for I'm going to your house today."*

When Jesus stopped by the sycamore-fig, the hidden Zacchaeus would have naturally tensed, or maybe even experienced a quick sweat. And then, sheer terror would have gripped his soul as Jesus (and the crowd) lifted their eyes. He braced to be a further spectacle of ridicule—especially as Jesus called him by name—"Zacchaeus."

But in Jesus' use of his personal name there is the hint of grace. The same all-knowing eyes that earlier had seen Nathanael under a fig tree and discerned his guileless character, now saw Zacchaeus and his guilty character, and called him, just as he had called Nathanael, to himself (cf. John 1:47–49). It was supernatural knowledge given Jesus for that moment by the Father. And then, as Jesus invited himself to Zacchaeus's home, He did not say, "I would like to stay at your house," but *I must stay.*[7] Jesus regarded His encounter with Zacchaeus as His divine mission. His seeking Zacchaeus was a work of sovereign grace.

What we begin to see at this point in the story is that Zacchaeus's seeking of Jesus and Jesus' seeking of Zacchaeus are both a sovereign work

> # BY GRACE, THE LITTLE MAN HAD BECOME HUGE!

of God. The crossing of their lives at the sycamore was a work of divine providence. This meeting was set before the foundation of the world (cf. Ephesians 1:4–6). The camel was about to go through the eye of a needle!

Luke says, "So he came down at once and welcomed him gladly" (19:6). The glad leap with which Zacchaeus dismounted the tree, twigs and leaves flying, may have revealed to Zacchaeus himself, as it no doubt did to the bystanders, what it was that he had been dimly wishing for.[8] From here on, apart from the crowd's muttering, "He has gone to be the guest of a 'sinner'" (v. 7), there is only joy—Zacchaeus's joy and Jesus' joy.

## DIVINE TRANSFORMATION

To the crowd's amazement, off strode Jesus with the half-pint kingpin of the Jericho tax machine hurrying alongside on his busy legs. Jesus and His disciples would spend the night there according to Palestinian custom. And sometime during that stay, probably after much discussion and prayer, a little big man would formally stand and declare for all Jericho to hear, "Look, Lord! Here and now I give half of my possessions to the poor, and if I have cheated anybody out of anything, I will pay back four times the amount" (19:8).

What an enormous divestment! For starters, Zacchaeus gave away 50 percent of his wealth to the poor. And, then, from the remaining 50 percent he pledged to make restitution of four times the amount of what he had extorted. The "if" implies that he had cheated many people—and placed his entire fortune in jeopardy.[9] In effect, he lived out the command that had earlier caused the Rich Ruler so much grief: "Sell everything you have and give to the poor, and you will have treasure in heaven. Then come, follow me" (18:22). He was walking through the eye of a needle—and living to tell about it.

By grace, the little man had become huge! Acceptance by God had given the tax collector what he had vainly sought for in the accumulation of wealth—wholeness and satisfaction. The compulsive drive to make money was gone. He no longer needed his wealth. He went in mastered by the passion to get; he left mastered by the passion to give. He went in the littlest man in Jericho; he left the biggest man in town. Something had happened inside that house with Jesus.

## DIVINE DECLARATION

We don't have to guess what Jesus' declaration to Zacchaeus sounded like. "Jesus said to him, 'Today salvation has come to this house, because this man, too, is a son of Abraham'" (19:9). The liberating joy of salvation was coursing through his soul. By faith, Zacchaeus had become a true son of Abraham. He shared the faith and works of Abraham (cf. Romans 2:28–29; 4:1–16; Galatians 3:13–14; John 8:39–40).[10] In Jesus, he had met the "horn of salvation," prophesied right before Jesus' birth who would "give his people the knowledge of salvation through the forgiveness of their sins" (Luke 1:69, 77ff). Zacchaeus became a new man. That is why he gave away his earthly fortune.

Nonbelievers are quick to criticize the Gospel as sentimental and unpractical, using a number of ugly adjectives. But, if it is impractical, it is our fault—not the Gospel's. The demands of the Gospel are intensely practical, and they include a reorientation to one's material possessions. Listen to Luke's gospel, "But woe to you who are rich, for you have already received your comfort" (6:24).

Jesus pronounces a woe on the rich because in their self-sufficiency they are the opposite of those to whom He came to preach the Gospel—as He said at the onset, "The Spirit of the Lord is on me, because he has anointed me to preach good news to the poor" (Luke 4:18).

Luke 12:20–21 bears these solemn words to all who trust in riches, "But God said to him, 'You fool! This very night your life will be demanded from you. Then who will get what you have prepared for yourself?' This is how it will be with anyone who stores up things for himself but is not rich toward God."

Luke 16:13 records Jesus' material/spiritual axiom: "No servant can serve two masters. Either he will hate the one and love the other, or he will be devoted to the one and despise the other. You cannot serve both God and Money."

Jesus is saying over and over that it is useless to talk about loving Him and trusting Him, and having the sweet assurance of forgiveness, and the glorious hope of heaven, unless it makes a difference in our material attachments. Strong emotion, deep sweet feelings, confidence in forgiveness are wonderful only if they open our hands in the graced giving of ourselves.

You may have reached a sticking point in your spiritual development, and you wonder why. You read your Bible. Your language has changed, and you're more honest than before. But give to the church regularly and generously? Well, you're not quite ready.

Zacchaeus was ready because he was regenerated. He was ready because he was enlarged; he was a big man. The Gospel makes little men big. As we mentioned, the account ends with the grand summary of Christ's mission, "For the Son of Man came to seek and to save what was lost" (19:10). Zacchaeus was beyond salvation. You would have felt this way about him if you had lived in Jericho. You would have written him off. He had turned his back on God's Word and His covenant people. He was a perpetrator of the Roman oppression, a traitor. He made his money off the backs of his own people, like a pimp. His cartel was the cause of much injustice. He was the baddest and meanest (and littlest) man in town.

Salvation would normally be impossible for such a man. Only one thing saved Zacchaeus; the Son of Man graciously sought him out. "Son of Man" is the name for the majestic being of Daniel's vision to whom the Ancient of Days has given all dominion and authority (cf. Daniel 7:13–14). "Son of Man" is also the name that prophesied the Incarnation, because God the Son became like a son of man. This is the transcendent God-man, coeternal with the Ancient of Days, who sought Zacchaeus—and did the impossible. Camel-brained, dromedary-souled Zacchaeus passed through the eye of a needle not as a "long bloody thread from tail to snout," but ultimately because of the blood of Jesus, the Door (cf. John 10:9 KJV).

Salvation came to Zacchaeus because he was sought-out. It was God who prompted the interior longing in Zacchaeus. As Augustine said of God in another place, "You follow close behind the fugitive and recall us to Yourself in ways we cannot understand" (Bk. IV, 4).[11] He makes us hungry. He causes us to search. He compels us to come. At the end of C. S. Lewis's spiritual biography he writes: "The words *compelle intrare,* compel them to come in, have been so abused by wicked men that we shudder at them; but, properly understood, they plumb the depth of the Divine mercy. The hardness of God is kinder than the softness of men, and His compulsion is our liberation."[12]

> # IS GOD SEEKING YOU?

It was God who orchestrated the interior compulsion for Zacchaeus to seek Jesus, and the exterior crossing of their lives at the fig tree. Zacchaeus was caught because in his seeking he was sought.

*I sought the Lord, and afterward I knew*
*He moved my heart to seek Him, seeking me;*

*It was not I that found, O Savior true;*
*No, I was found of Thee.*[13]

Is God seeking you? If so, you will know it by an interior dis-ease. Nothing satisfies and that goes for the most privileged delights. The greater your material wealth, the less you are satisfied. You are never really comfortable. You lack wholeness. You lack a clear conscience. You lack peace. But understand this: "The hardness of God is kinder than the softness of men, and His compulsion is our liberation."[14] This is Christ seeking you. This is grace.

And, if that is so, then you are at the sycamore-fig— and He is saying, "Come down, I want to dine with you. I want your soul. I have sought you. I am seeking you. I am the Son of Man. I am an awesome God. I died for you. Come down!"

But you say, "I'm too small. If You knew my heart, You wouldn't say that!" And He says, "I will give you a new heart, a big heart. I will show you a better place to store your true treasure. Come with Me."

Will you come?

# NOTES

1. Bob L. Ross, *A Pictorial Biography of C.H. Spurgeon* (Pilgrim, Pasadena, TX: 1974), 85, 88.
2. John Nolland, *Word Bible Commentary, Vol. 35b, Luke 9:21–18:34* (Dallas: Word, 1993), 903, 907.
3. Geoffrey W. Bromiley, trans., *Theological Dictionary of the New Testament, Vol. 8* (Grand Rapids: Eerdman's, 1976), 98.
4. C. S. Lewis, *Poems* (New York: Harcourt Brace Jovanovich, 1977), 134.
5. R.S. Pine-Coffin, trans., *Saint Augustine Confessions* (London: Penguin, 1961), 144.
6. J. D. Douglas, ed., *The New Bible Dictionary* (Grand Rapids: Eerdmans, 1962), 1294.
7. Leon Morris, *Luke* (Grand Rapids: Eerdmans, 1988), 298.
8. Alexander Maclaren, *Expositions of Holy Scriptures* (Grand Rapids: Eerdmans, 1974), 156.
9. I. H. Marshall, *The Gospel of Luke* (Grand Rapids: Eerdmans, 1978), 698.
10. E. Earle Ellis, *The Gospel of Luke* (Grand Rapids: Eerdmans, 1974), 220, 221.
11. *Confessions*, 75.
12. C. S. Lewis, *Surprised by Joy* (New York: Harcourt, Brace & World, n.d.), 229.
13. D. A. Carson and John D. Woodbridge, *Letters Along the Way* (Wheaton, IL: Crossway, 1993), 36.
14. Lewis, *Surprised by Joy,* 229.

## FOR FURTHER REFERENCE

1. Humanly speaking, why was Zacchaeus not a likely candidate for the kingdom?

2. Why was the encounter between Jesus and Zacchaeus a work of sovereign grace? Name the interior and exterior factors.

3. Can you recall the inner and outer workings of grace when you came to Christ? List them in separate columns. This may be difficult if your conversion came when you were a child. But it will be good for your soul to attempt this.

4. What do these Scriptures tell us about Zacchaeus and us—apart from Christ? Look up Romans 3:10–18 and Ephesians 2:1–3.

5. What do the Scriptures tell us about grace? Look up Ephesians 2:4–9; Romans 3:22–23 and 11:6; Matthew 11:27; and 2 Corinthians 4:6.

6. Zacchaeus was curious about Jesus and was being directed by a sense of emptiness within him to know Christ. Do you feel that your life is somehow empty? What created this feeling? Is Christ the answer to filling your emptiness?

# *your* HEART'S EARS

I have great sympathy for Eutychus, the young man who fell asleep while Paul was preaching and who, unfortunately, was sitting on the sill of a third-floor window from which he fell to his death—and then was raised by Paul. I feel sorry for Eutychus on several counts. First, he fell asleep on the apostle Paul. Second, because he was in such a place that it had such unhappy results. And third, because Luke was there to write down the whole embarrassing account!

There is one thing I am sure of after forty years in the ministry: On any given Sunday there are those who are in danger of falling asleep in church. You would be amazed at what preachers can see. It's natural to feel that you are safe in the anonymity of the congregation. Not so! I have seen people fall asleep and bump their heads on the pew in front of them. I have heard people waken with a snort. I have been sitting on the platform when one of my associates dozed off and dropped his hymnal.

In one congregation there was a young man who sat on the front row and slept every Sunday. As soon as I was through the introduction, his eyes closed, head tilted. The most memorable instance of this was the Sunday both he and his wife fell asleep with their heads propped against one another. I have heard a preacher tell of an elder who fell asleep, and when his wife nudged him, he stood and pronounced the benediction.

I say all this because I have great empathy for those who have trouble staying awake in church. Some of you work such trying schedules that when you sit down in church, it's the first time you have relaxed all week. Others are sometimes the victims of medication. Sometimes the sermon is boring. I know—as the preacher I have listened to it twice!

Falling asleep in church really doesn't concern me. It can happen for any number of reasons, both good and bad. What does concern me are the thousands who warm a pew every Lord's Day with their bodies awake and their souls asleep. In biblical terms—"though hearing, they do not hear" (Matthew 13:13).

Jesus was well aware of this when he preached the parable of the sower to the largest crowd yet in His ministry. The multitude was so vast that He had to take to the water and preach from a boat (cf. Mark 4:1). Beautifully, the acoustics of the floating pulpit enhanced the people's hearing. The people sat in a great arc on the rising shore so that each person could see Jesus against the dazzling turquoise backdrop of the sea and perfectly hear the Savior's words as they resonated across the water. No healthy ear could miss hearing Jesus' grand words. Yet when He finished He began to call out, "He who has ears to hear, let him hear" (Luke 8:8). Jesus' plaintive refrain echoed and reechoed across the waters.

Think of it! Jesus was the Word incarnate, God's ultimate communication. And here, we see that His very fiber longed for His hearer to comprehend His words.

## HARD SAYING

Though all heard Jesus' amazing teaching, many kinds of hearing took place that day. Some half-listened. Some tuned Him out. Some listened and understood. Others listened but were confused. Some of His followers were in the dark themselves and, challenged by Jesus' ringing call to listen, they began by asking Him about the parable (8:9). Jesus therefore graciously responded with one of His famous "hard sayings." "The knowledge of the secrets of the kingdom of God has been given to you, but to others I speak in parables so that, 'though seeing, they may not see; though hearing, they may not understand'" (8:10).

What did Jesus' mysterious pronouncement mean? The sixth chapter of Isaiah tells us, because Jesus' hard saying quotes from it. There we have the famous account of Isaiah's stunning encounter with God in the temple. Chapter six opens with the dramatic scene. "In the year that King Uzziah died, I saw the Lord seated on a throne, high and exalted, and the train of his robe filled the temple" (Isaiah 6:1). The outcome of this holy confrontation was Isaiah's call and his acceptance, "Then I heard the voice of the Lord saying, 'Whom shall I send? And who will go for us?' And I said, 'Here am I. Send me!'" (v. 8).

Then follows the oddest commission perhaps ever given to a prophet. Isaiah is told to charge the people not to understand, and that he is to make their hearts hard:

*"Go and tell this people: 'Be ever hearing, but never understanding; be ever seeing, but never perceiving.' Make the heart of this people calloused; make their ears dull and close their eyes. Otherwise they might see with their eyes, hear with their ears, understand with their hearts, and turn and be healed." (vv. 9–10)*

How did Isaiah obey this strange commission? By beginning to preach with obscure expressions and complex reasoning? By becoming a "mist in the pulpit" so there would be a "fog in the pew"? On the contrary, Isaiah's preaching was purposely plain, systematic, and reasoned. In fact, "the sophisticates of his day scorned him as fit only to conduct a kindergarten."[1] They disdained his simple preaching, saying, "Who is it he is trying to teach? To whom is he explaining his message? To children weaned from their milk, to those just taken from the breast?" (Isaiah 28:9).

In actual fact Isaiah fulfilled his commission to blind and harden the people by clearly preaching the truth. And when they rejected it he preached it again in the simplest form possible, so that their repeated rejections effected an increased hardness of heart.

> # YOUR HEART IS PERFECTLY REPRESENTED BY ONE OF THE FOUR SOILS.

Further light on Jesus' hard saying is provided by the parallel account of the soils in Matthew 13:12–13 which also references Isaiah 6, explaining, "Whoever has will be given more, and he will have an abundance. Whoever does not have, even what he has will be taken from him. This is why I speak to them in parables: Though seeing, they do not see; though hearing, they do not hear or understand."

By this Jesus was saying that the condition of your heart determines its receptivity to truth. Many people, especially the religious leaders, long since turned from the original intent of Scripture, had heard straightfor-

ward teaching from Jesus that they rejected. Thus the little truth they still understood could ultimately be lost—
even that would be taken away from them. Those who
receive truth and act upon it will receive more. Those
who reject truth will ultimately lose the bit they have.
The parables were full of truth, but for truth-rejecting
people, they became increasingly dark.

This principle is seen in other areas of our lives. Physically, if we fail to exercise a muscle, we will one day lose
its use. It is the same with our mental powers. If we fail
to use them, there will come a time when we will not be
able to summon their full strength.

Actually God's Word demands even more than listening. *It demands doing.* If we consider ourselves believers,
we must set ourselves to always respond to God's truth as
we read it or hear it from another believer or from the
pulpit. An excellent spiritual discipline is to respond to
God's truth with action, be it ever so small. "Do it or lose
it!" is an axiom that functions with unremitting vengeance,
or unremitting blessing.

## THE FOUR HEARTS

Alone with His followers (cf. Mark 4:10), after having
made His "hard-word," Jesus graciously explained the
parable. He told them that there were, and are, four
kinds of hearts that hear God's Word: a *hard* heart, a
*shallow* heart, an *infested* heart, and a *good* heart. These
four hearts were present in the large crowd that listened
to Jesus that day, and they are present in every large
assembly of the church today. In fact your heart is perfectly represented by one of the four soils. You are one of
them. As you now read through Jesus' astonishing explanation, humbly pray that you will have ears to hear.
Remember, "faith comes from hearing, and hearing
through the word of Christ" (Romans 10:17 ESV).

**Hard hearts.**

The Lord began by explaining about the seed cast along the path. "This is the meaning of the parable: The seed is the word of God. Those along the path are the ones who hear, and then the devil comes and takes away the word from their hearts, so that they may not believe and be saved" (Luke 8:11–12). The farmers' fields in ancient Palestine were long, narrow, often serpentine strips divided by paths that became beaten as hard as pavement by the feet, hooves, and wheels of those who used them.[2] The seeds merely bounced along these paths and were swept back and forth by the winds of nature and commerce.

These hard, beaten paths are emblematic of the everyday people who hear God's Word. The footfall of their own busy comings and goings and the incessant traffic of life have so hardened them that nothing of God's truth stirs them. When challenged by thoughts regarding man's origin and destiny, they dismiss it as "too hard." The same method is applied to Scripture's declarations about death and eternity—"Headache stuff!" Sin? "Everybody does it. So why should I be concerned?"

So life, for many, is no more than a sports page and a beer, or a fishing pole, or a movie magazine and an hour at the beauty shop, or a spin in the car. There may be no gross sin, but neither is there interest in God or His Word at all. Life is crowded with too many other things.

> *Into this world to eat and to sleep,*
> *And to know no reason why he was born.*
> *Save to consume the corn,*
> *Devour the cattle, flock and fish,*
> *And leave behind an empty dish.*
>
> (source unknown)

Some of these hardhearted may be more sophisticated. They have drunk freely from a loose set of attitudes and ideas known as modernity. They are not interested in God's Word because they don't believe that objective truth can be known. They worship technology's brilliance, and substitute it for God. They rarely ever pursue the logical end of their own presuppositions. They may be hostile to the Gospel message placed before them, but very often they are simply uninterested. Their hearts are as hard as Kryptonite and dulled to feeling by the busy pounding feet of life.

As the truth bounces on the hardened surface of their lives, Satan descends onto the scene with a fluttering interest, some busy excitement perhaps, or maybe some gossip to derail the potential believer, then flies away with the life-giving seed.

To reach this group, the hard ground needs to be broken up. Most often, the plowing that is needed is some pain or stress or trial to soften the hardness of their lives to the seed of God's truth. This is how grace has come to so many of our lives, isn't it? Difficulties made us quit our spirit-dulling busyness, and then the Word of God fell powerfully into the broken ground of our lives. Some of the hard hearts you know need to be plowed by sorrow and disappointment so that God's Word might take root. We must pray for this grace.

### Shallow hearts

Next our Lord offered explanation about the seed sown on rock. "Those on the rock are the ones who receive the word with joy when they hear it, but they have no root. They believe for a while, but in the time of testing they fall away" (8:13). In Palestine much of the land is a thin two- or three-inch veneer of soil over limestone bedrock. Here some of the seed fell, where the warm sun quickly heated the seed in the shallow soil, so that the seeds sprouted in feverish growth. But then the sun continued to beat down, and the plants' roots hit bedrock, where they withered and died. We've all observed the same sight in the quick death of grass on the shallow shoulders of expressways.

I have seen this withering effect take tragic toll in a number of lives over the years. On one occasion I saw a young man make a dazzling profession of Christ. In a few weeks he was speaking unbidden everywhere, dominating testimony meetings, reproving older Christians for their coldness. But then he broke his leg, cursed God and His people for his condition, attempted vindictive litigation on the innocent property owner, and abruptly fell away.

> # CERTAINLY AUTHENTIC FAITH INVOLVES GREAT EMOTION.

In retrospect, the problem was that he had had a shallow emotional response to Christ that never truly penetrated his heart. When affliction came, there was immediate rejection; the greening ceased. I am convinced that this is where so many enemies of the faith are shaped. Too many, through their emotion, have tasted something of God's power, but not true conversion—"half-Christians" we might say. In falling away they became bitter and jaundiced, and terribly lost.

Affliction, like the sun, brings growth to roots in good soil, but withers the shallow profession of faith. Helmut Thielicke, one of the great minds and personalities of evangelical Christianity, aptly comments:

> *There is nothing more cheering than trans-*
> *formed Christian people and there is nothing*
> *more disintegrating than people who have been*
> *merely "brushed" by Christianity, people who*
> *have been sown with a thousand seeds but in*
> *whose lives there is no depth and no rootage.*
> *Therefore, they fall when the first whirlwind*
> *comes along. It is the half-Christians who*
> *always flop in the face of the first catastrophe*
> *that happens, because their dry intellectuality*
> *and their superficial emotionalism do not stand*
> *the test. So even that which they think they*
> *have is taken away from them. This is the wood*
> *from which the anti-Christians too are cut.*

> *They are almost always former half-Christians.*
> *A person who lets Jesus only halfway into his*
> *heart is far poorer than a one hundred percent*
> *worldling.*[3]

Certainly authentic faith involves great emotion. If there is no emotion, it is crippled faith and may be bogus. But true faith puts down deep sustaining roots in the mind and the will.

There are half-Christians reading this book right now. This is God's grace, because this book is for you. You had an emotional response to God's Word, a temporary greening of the soul. Perhaps you were congratulated. Perhaps some well-meaning but ill-advised person told you, "Now you're a Christian. Don't let anyone tell you otherwise." But you shriveled long ago when hard times came. There is no real life. And perhaps no one knows it but you, because it's easy to affect Christianness. If so, you need help. Your soul needs a doctor. You need to seek out a trusted Christian now.

## Infested hearts

Next Jesus explained the image of the sower casting his seed among the thorns. "The seed that fell among thorns stands for those who hear, but as they go on their way they are choked by life's worries, riches and pleasures, and they do not mature" (8:14). Here the thorn bushes are not visible in the soil because they have been burned off the surface, but their roots are intact. When the seed is sown on this soil, then watered and germinated, the entrenched thorns also sprout and grow with a virulent violence, choking out the grain before it can produce fruit.

The thorns, Jesus explained, represented "life's worries, riches and pleasures." This portrayed a divided heart, infested by irreconcilable loyalties. This heart makes gestures toward Christ, but "life's worries" draw it back. It is pulled in other directions, leaving no room for authentic spiritual concern. Life's "riches and pleasures" draw this heart back from life. "Keeping up with the Joneses" is where life is! That is:

> *Buying things*
> *you do not need*
> *to impress people*
> *you do not like*
> *with money*
> *you do not have.*

In many ways this is a perfect description of a suburban heart.

It is a lost heart. A heart that is overcome with a love for "riches and pleasure" is not a believing heart. As Jesus explained in the Sermon on the Mount, "No one can serve two masters. Either he will hate the one and love the other, or he will be devoted to the one and despise the other. You cannot serve both God and Money" (Matthew 6:24). Many began well, and it looked like they were believers, but the love for the world and worries over the things and pleasures of this life has strangled all vestiges of life from their souls.

Some of you reading these lines have weed-infested, divided, suburban hearts. It is not for others to judge, but inside there is no question about what you really love. You need to be honest with yourself for your soul's sake.

## Good hearts

Finally there is the good soil in which the seed brings forth fruit. Jesus said, "But the seed on good soil stands for those with a noble and good heart, who hear the word, retain it, and by persevering produce a crop" (8:15). The seed of God's Word does not bounce off the hard surface of this heart. Neither does it temporarily flourish in the shallow soil of emotion, only to shrivel under adversity. Nor is it divided by its competing desires and strangled. It is a heart that allows God's Word to take deep root in it. It produces then a harvest of good character: "But the fruit of the Spirit is love, joy, peace, patience, kindness, goodness, faithfulness, gentleness and self-control" (Galatians 5:22–23). This is followed by a bounty of good works, as the heart is remade by Christ Jesus for good works (cf. Ephesians 2:10).

The hearing and reception of God's Word is a mystery, and this great parable has graced us with insight into what is going on with those who sit under the Word. There is no doubt as to what true hearing is: It is a heart that hears and does God's Word. Luke shares Christ's passion that we understand this, and so our theologian/author links two brief supporting paragraphs to this to make the point.

## THE LAMP

The first is the mini-parable of the lamp: "No one lights a lamp and hides it in a jar or puts it under a bed. Instead, he puts it on a stand, so that those who come in can see the light. For there is nothing hidden that will not be disclosed, and nothing concealed that will not be known or brought out into the open" (Luke 8:16–17).

Jesus depicts His followers, who hear and receive the Word as lamps. His point is that they must let the light that is in them shine forth to illumine others.[4] They must shine the light now, so that the people will receive it, and thus be prepared for the judgment when all will be revealed. This makes their present listening to the Word everything. So Jesus caps the parable: "Therefore consider carefully how you listen. Whoever has will be given more; whoever does not have, even what he thinks he has will be taken from him" (8:18). It is the same teaching of Isaiah 6, which He referenced earlier—do it or lose it! Hearing involves doing. And, humanly speaking, the spread of the light of the Gospel in this world is dependent upon Jesus' hearers doing His Word. Happily, the more they do it, the more light they will receive.

## JESUS' "FAMILY"

Lastly, Luke drives the great point home by relating an incident involving Jesus and his family: "Now Jesus' mother and brothers came to see him, but they were not able to get near him because of the crowd. Someone told him, 'Your mother and brothers are standing outside, wanting to see you.' He replied, 'My mother and brothers are those who hear God's word and put it into practice'" (vv. 19–21)— literally—"who hear the Word of God and do it." So there we have it. You and I are Jesus' family if we hear and do His Word. Hearing and doing His Word is key to intimacy with God. His blood runs in our veins, so to speak, if we hear and do His Word.

## Hear!

Whatever the condition of your heart, whether it be hard, shallow, infested, or good, you must listen with all you have to God's Word when it is read privately and publicly and proclaimed. When it comes to listening to preaching, the example of Dietrich Bonhoeffer the martyr has helped me personally. Bonhoeffer ran an underground seminary for theological students during the oppressive years of Nazi Germany. He was a very intelligent man who possessed immense critical capabilities. But in his preaching classes as he listened to his students expound God's Holy Word, he always set aside his pencil and listened intently with his Bible open before him—no matter how poor the sermon was. He believed that the preaching of God's Word ought to be attended as if he were listening to the very voice of God. That is how you must listen: always looking to the text, always engaged, always thinking, always praying. Jesus has called us to do so.

## Do!

But hearing is no good, if it does not eventuate in doing. Isaiah and Jesus are clear: Do it or lose it! Every attention to God's Word must be coupled with the willingness to do it; otherwise the truth of it will fade. If you hear God's Word, and you are impressed that you must forgive another, you must do it. Otherwise, the Word of forgiveness may be taken away.

Has His Word impressed you that you must forgive? Do it! Has His Word impressed you that you must confess a wrongdoing? Do it! Has His Word impressed you that you must apologize? Do it! Has His Word impressed you that you must speak the truth regardless of the consequences? Do it! Has His Word impressed you that you must discontinue a certain practice? Do it! Has His Word impressed you that you must make a gift? Do it! Has His Word impressed you that you must bear witness to an acquaintance? Do it! Has His Word impressed you that you must leave all to serve Him? Do it!

If in reading this chapter you have come to realize that you're one of the soils other than the good soil—that you are either *hard* or *shallow* or *infested*—then it is apparent that God's Word is really speaking to you and that you are in the way of grace. Now, you need to *do* His Word. Jesus said, "The work of God is this: to believe in the one he has sent" (John 6:29). Do it! "Believe in the Lord Jesus, and you will be saved" (Acts 16:31).

# NOTES

1. J. A. Motyer, *The Prophecy of Isaiah* (Leicester, England: InterVarsity, 1993), 79.
2. William Barclay, *The Gospel of Mark* (Philadelphia: Westminster, 1956), 91–92.
3. Helmut Thielicke, *The Waiting Father* (New York: Harper & Row, 1975), 57.
4. Leon Morris, *Luke* (Grand Rapids: Eerdmans, 1975), 168.

## FOR FURTHER REFERENCE

1. Jesus' parable of the soils/hearts describes the effects of Scripture as it is sown amongst humanity. Think back to the first time you heard the Gospel preached. Did it "bounce off" of you, or did it take root and grow? What type of soil is your heart today?

2. Think of a couple of people you know who have heard the Gospel message preached and have not truly come to Christ. Which of the four soils would you consider their hearts to be like? Why?

3. Why does the fourth soil alone describe the heart of a true believer?

4. How does God graciously soften the soil of hard hearts?

5. How does the saying "Do it or lose it" apply to hearing God's Word?

# *narrow*
# IS WIDE

A few years ago, I attended a convocation of ministers in Cambridge, Massachusetts, where one of the plenary speakers experienced a heartening encounter as he was preparing his message. He had risen early and found a restaurant next to Harvard Yard where he could apply the "finishing touches." As he worked, he saw the town awaken, and the restaurant fill with an array of weird and wonderful people. From their appearance, some had obviously slept in the street the previous night. Others, casually dressed students and greying professors, were apparently regulars of the restaurant.

He was out of his element. He felt decidedly uncomfortable in this mass of sophisticated and gritty humanity. The comfort zone of his own pastoral world seemed as remote as Mars amidst this humanist, I-want-God-on-my-terms backdrop. It was a world of intellectual supremacy and egalitarian ideals, where reason prevailed over simple belief. And yet the apparent contradictions of reason and equality—desperate, impoverished souls—sat side-by-side with resident intellectuals. The university culture was overwhelming, and he felt insignificant. He began to dwell upon his insignificance and how foolish the Gospel seemed in such a setting. He felt small.

But two things happened to encourage him. A sparrow landed on his table inside the restaurant and looked him over, and he thought of Christ's words about sparrows. Then he looked across the aisle and saw a young Asian woman intently reading a book. He watched further and saw that she was studying the Scriptures. Encouraged by the spark of spirituality in this cosmopolitan coffee shop, he spoke to her asking, "I see that you are reading the Bible. Are you a Christian?" She smiled and replied, "Oh yes. I've found the narrow way."

Her answer was remarkable. Neither he (nor I for that matter) in all our years in ministry had ever heard anyone answer like that. In the ensuing conversation she explained that she had come from Korea to study at Harvard, and that she was the only Christian from her family. Here was a young Christian woman, ten thousand miles away from her Buddhist home (with its three million gods, the antithesis of the "narrow way") in the midst of Harvard's aggressive pluralism (which tolerates everything except "narrowness") who so profoundly understood her Christian faith that she expressed it with unabashed acumen as "the narrow way."

As you would expect, my preacher friend, Alistair Begg, was profoundly encouraged that morning to preach the Word—which he then did with memorable effect. This young student understood and had appropriated a kingdom truth that is glossed over by many, especially if they live in a congenial Christian subculture —that the entrance into God's kingdom is narrow.

Christians in America today are challenged by the concept of the narrow door. Our culture says we should embrace ideas through a wide portal, allowing many concepts to flood into our lives. Our faith is no exception to this trend. As a result, many believers have been fed a diet of pluralistic notions that suggest that there are

many roads to heaven, or that Christians should be toler-
ant of many practices because there are no absolute
truths. These influences have greatly weakened the
church because they have weakened the faith of believers. The post-modern, no-absolute-truth model has challenged the faith of so many believers, that they don't
know if they're coming or going, to heaven that is. Many
of their spiritual teachers are in the same sad state.

Many churchgoers appear to be Christians on the
outside—they go to church regularly, tithe, support min-
istries—but on the inside, they are unsure of what they
believe. Their spiritual substance is very shallow. They
are the "unchurched
Christians," people
on the edge of the
kingdom, but lacking
that firm connection
that will bring them
humbly and with
unquestioning grati-
tude into the arms of
the Father.

> # JEWS IN JESUS' DAY PRESUMED SALVATION BY PRIVILEGE.

Jesus had to deal
with many such people as He discussed the great matter
of eternity with the Father. The occasion for Jesus' original setting forth of this truth on the road to Jerusalem
was a question from an unnamed person in the crowd,
"Lord, are only a few people going to be saved?"
(Luke13:23).

It was a smug, self-complacent question because the
general understanding among the Jews was that all Jews
would be saved except the very worst. The Mishnah was
explicit about this: "All Israelites have a share in the
world to come, for it is written, Thy people also shall be
all righteous, they shall inherit the land for ever; the
branch of my planting, the work of my hands that I may

be glorified. And these are they that have no share in the
world to come: he that says that there is no resurrection
of the dead prescribed in the Law, and [he that says] that
the Law is not from Heaven, and an Epicurean" (San-
hedrin 10.1).[1]

So when the question rang from the crowd, the hearers expected Jesus to affirm that all Jews would make it
through the pearly gates, unless they did some "big-time"
sins like the rebellion of Korah or that of Absalom. Along
with this, they thought, all the Gentiles would be
excluded from the kingdom except for a few proselytes
who followed in the tradition of Rahab and Ruth. The
question was a presumptive, "make us feel good" query
meant to solidify Jewish feelings of religious superiority.
It played to their elitist instincts.

Jesus' regard for the question can be seen in His
response, because He really didn't answer it, but responded
with a command, "Make every effort to enter through the
narrow door, because many, I tell you, will try to enter
and will not be able to" (v. 24).

Jesus had assaulted their complacency, because Jesus'
use of the word "many" meant "many of you Jews will try
to enter and will not be able to"—implying that a majority
of His hearers wouldn't make it! Their complacent notion
of a guaranteed ticket into heaven had received a stinging
slap, and uneasiness spread over His hearers.

Jews in Jesus' day presumed salvation by privilege.
They were privileged to be part of the covenant commu-
nity—they had the Law, the prophets, the temple, and a
history of privilege—so they assumed salvation as a
given. It was fatal thinking. Paul later attacked such presumption in his letter to the Romans:

*Now you, if you call yourself a Jew; if you rely on
the law and brag about your relationship to God; if
you know his will and approve of what is superior*

*because you are instructed by the law; if you are
convinced that you are a guide for the blind, a light
for those who are in the dark, an instructor of the
foolish, a teacher of infants, because you have in
the law the embodiment of knowledge and truth—
you, then, who teach others, do you not teach
yourself? (2:17–21)*

His point was this: Your Jewish privilege had better
make a difference, or it is all for nothing. Sadly, many
were lost then, and subsequently.

Jesus sustained this warning in His kingdom parables, in the parable of the soils where the seed fell on
three of the four soils in vain. The parable of the soils
taught that many professing "believers" would be lost
(cf. Luke 8:1–15). Likewise in the parable of the sheep
and the goats, the great flock will be divided, and a large
contingent of goats will be sent off to eternal punishment
(cf. Matthew 25:31–46). Privileged presumption charac-
terizes many of the lost in this parable.

Presumption of salvation through privilege continues
to delude multitudes in the professing church today,
especially those who come from Christian homes. And
Jesus' "many . . . will try to enter and will not be able to"
applies with the same urgency. Jesus does not wish to
inject false fears into our minds, but He would have us
examine our lives that they might be put away.

## THE NARROW DOOR

Jesus represented the way of salvation as "the narrow
door." It is a moral image suggesting the spiritual posture of the person who strives to enter the kingdom. The
imagery is similar to that of a camel passing through the
needle's eye, and pictures the difficulty of facing up to
the demands of Jesus in self-denial.[2]

The passage to heaven is not through the great portal of a palace, but by a narrow, low door, through which one must humbly squeeze. And after entering, the road remains narrow, as Jesus explained when He preached another time, "Enter through the narrow gate. For wide is the gate and broad is the road that leads to destruction, and many enter through it. But small is the gate and narrow the road that leads to life, and only a few find it" (Matthew 7:13–14).

Few people are willing to assume the humble posture and shed what is necessary to get through the gate, and fewer still are willing to tread the narrow road. Few are willing to do as does that remarkable Korean student— reading her Bible for all her university world to see as she embraces "the narrow way."

### THE AGONY

The Lord's call in Luke 13:24 to "make every effort to enter" or "strive to enter" (KJV) is the Greek word *agonizomai,* from which our word *agonize* is derived. Agony suggests the kind of moral struggle necessary to enter the kingdom. "We are not saved by effort, but we shall not believe without effort" (Alexander Maclaren).[3]

In light of what is at stake (heaven or hell) and its eternal implications, we cannot strive enough to get through the narrow door. It must be sought with everything we have. The wisdom of God's Word must be mined with fervor like prospectors during the Gold Rush. Our prayers ought to be perpetual.

> *"Do not work for food that spoils, but for food that endures to eternal life, which the Son of Man will give you. On him God the Father has placed his seal of approval." Then they asked him, "What must we do to do the works God requires?" Jesus*

*answered, "The work of God is this: to believe in
the one he has sent." (John 6:27–29)*

If entry into God's glorious kingdom is not a sure
thing, despite our outward trappings of faith, then we
must put ourselves out to believe; we must agonize over
entrance into the kingdom.

## A CLOSED DOOR

There is inevitably a time limit on the offer of salvation, as Jesus makes so ominously clear. "Once the owner
of the house gets up and closes the door, you will stand
outside knocking and pleading" (v. 25a). The message for
every living soul who hears these words is: the gate is
open right now! The fact that you can read these words
in your mortal flesh means that you can respond, if you
so wish. When your body is gone, so will be the opportu-
nity. "Man is destined to die once, and after that to face
judgment" (Hebrews 9:27). But you're alive. Therefore
the door is not slammed for you. "Now is the day of salvation" (2 Corinthians 6:2).

Eventually the narrow door will be slammed, shut by
either death or the Lord's return—ushering in eternal
tragedy on those who have not entered as is portrayed in
the tiny prophetic dialogue:

> *"Sir, open the door for us."
> But he will answer,
> "I don't know you or where you come from."
> Then you will say,
> "We ate and drank with you,
>   and you taught in our streets."
> But he will reply,
>   "I don't know you or where you come from.*

*Away from me, all you evildoers!"*
*(Luke 13:25–27)*

Two complementary things have kept them out of the kingdom. First, they have no personal relationship with the master. Twice he issues a categorical denial of relationship. "I don't know you or where you come from." It is a total, utter denial despite the fact that they argue, "We ate and drank with you, and you taught in our streets" (v. 26). None of the crowd could persuade the master to accept that their superficial knowledge of him had established a relationship. They were total strangers.

Nor will such arguments work today. Some may argue that they have eaten and drunk with Christ at the Lord's Table and heard His Word preached—in the pulpit of His church. This is all very good, but it does not establish relationship. Some who have never missed the Lord's table and the preaching of the Word will hear Him say, "I don't know you or where you are from." If attendance in the Lord's house and His memorials could save a soul, Caiaphas would be in glory. If hearing the Word is enough, then Herod would be in heaven.

In fact, "doing ministry" does not prove relationship. It is very significant that in the Sermon on the Mount, shortly after Jesus urges His hearers to enter through the narrow gate (Matthew 7:13–14), He warns: "Not everyone who says to me, 'Lord, Lord,' will enter the kingdom of heaven, but only he who does the will of my Father who is in heaven. Many will say to me on that day, 'Lord, Lord, did we not prophesy in your name, and in your name drive out demons and perform many miracles?' Then I will tell them plainly, 'I never knew you. Away from me, you evildoers!'" (7:21–23).

So we must understand that we may have been preachers and ministered to thousands; we may have been Sunday school teachers and pointed little ones to

Christ; we may have been missionaries and been held up as paragons of sacrifice, and for all that we may end up as castaways. Why? Because it is not mighty works that save us, but vital union with Christ by real faith.[4] So the burning question all of us must ask is, *Does Christ know me?* Are you in authentic relationship with Him?

The second, the corollary question: Has the relationship with Christ that you claim turned you from evil? Are you morally improved from God's point of view? Or will He say, "Away from me, you evildoer!" Notice, the telling question is not in terms of "ministry" or standing in the church, but in terms of authentic righteousness.

## A CLOSED FEAST

When Moses encountered God at the burning bush, God identified Himself as "the God of your father, the God of Abraham, the God of Isaac and the God of Jacob" (Exodus 3:6). They were the progenitors of Israel and representatives of the heroes of the Jewish people. So we can understand how horrifying Jesus' next sentence was to His hearers: "There will be weeping there, and gnashing of teeth, when you see Abraham, Isaac and Jacob and all the prophets in the kingdom of God, but you yourselves thrown out" (v. 28). "Weeping" indicates sorrow; "gnashing of teeth," fierce rage. Many Israelites would be cast out of glorified Israel.

But there is an even more exquisite misery—"People will come from east and west and north and south, and will take their places at the feast in the kingdom of God" (v. 29). While unbelieving Israel is cast out, Gentiles will sit down with the great trio and the house of Israel. Because they belong to Christ, they are in Paul's words "Abraham's seed, and heirs according to the promise" (Galatians 3:29). And they are not just there, but they are joyously feasting! Whom will they see? Abraham, Isaac, and Jacob and Dr. Luke and Timothy and Augustine? Who knows?

In fact, it may be the big three, and the prophets, and a bunch of "no name" Gentiles, because Jesus concluded, "Indeed there are those who are last who will be first, and first who will be last" (v. 30). Such is God's grace! Such is God's grace that they receive the same reward, just as the parable of the workers in the vineyard makes so clear when the master paid those who worked an hour the same as those who worked all day—joyously answering the daylong workers' objections:

> # THE NARROW WAY IS SPIRITUAL AND NOT HEREDITARY.

*"But he answered one of them, 'Friend, I am not being unfair to you. Didn't you agree to work for a denarius? Take your pay and go. I want to give the man who was hired last the same as I gave you. Don't I have the right to do what I want with my own money? Or are you envious because I am generous?' So the last will be first, and the first will be last." (Matthew 20:13–16)*

### NARROW BUT WIDE!

Perhaps you've noticed that Luke's "narrow door" text touches on one of Luke's grand themes: the universality of the Gospel—that it is for all people, Jews and Gentiles. Christ's words teach us that the kingdom is narrower than His Jewish hearers thought because they assumed that all Israel would just walk in. Jesus taught that many of them would not make it through the narrow door. The door's narrowness was moral. It demanded humility. It demanded moral decisions. And those who got through the door were those in relationship with God. God actually knew and knows them. Jesus would explain in His High Priestly Prayer, "Now this is eternal life: that they may know you, the only true God, and Jesus Christ, whom you have sent" (John 17:3). This relationship with God delivered them from evildoing.

Here's the ultimate beauty: *The narrowness of the kingdom has created a kingdom that is broader than we would ever have thought!* This is because the narrow way is spiritual and not hereditary, because it is a relationship with God which comes by faith, because it makes men and women new from the inside out, because it is all grace.

And because of this there is hope for you and me; there is hope for all Jews and Gentiles. There is hope for a Korean girl from a family of Buddhists. There is hope for a Hebrew of the Hebrews. There is hope for every shade of suburbanite and city-dweller. The narrow way is wide open to all.

Have you entered it? If not, Jesus says, "Make every effort to enter through the narrow door" (v. 24). We are not saved by effort, but we shall not believe without effort! It's not too late to be first.

# NOTES

1. Herbert Danby, trans., *The Mishnah* (London: Oxford, 1933), 397.
2. I. H. Marshall, *The Gospel of Luke* (Grand Rapids: Eerdmans, (1974), 565.
3. Alexander Maclaren, *The Epistles of St. Paul to the Colossians and Philemon, The Exposition Bible* (New York: A. C. Armstrong, 1903), 9.
4. C. H. Spurgeon, *The Metropolitan Tabernacle Pulpit, Vol. 8* (Pasadena, TX: Pilgrim, 1975), 582 from where the preceding two paragraphs have utilized Spurgeon's thoughts and phraseology.

## FOR FURTHER REFERENCE

1. The idea of a narrow way is offensive to today's culture. Why?

2. Is it fair or right that the door to God's kingdom is narrow? Wouldn't a loving God make it easier for everyone to enter? Why not?

3. How is it that we can hear Christ's message, but not be on the path to the narrow door? What obstacles sidetrack us or derail us as we seek Him? How can we get back on track?

4. Jesus said, "I am the way and the truth and the life. No one comes to the Father except through me" (John 14:6). How is this narrow? And, how is this wide?

5. What is the key to reaching the narrow door? Who stops us from entering—God or we ourselves?

6. Have you entered the narrow door?

# *from* DEATH VALLEY

S ome years ago when I was a youth pastor, I hiked with some of my high schoolers to the top of Mount Whitney in California, which is the highest spot in the continental United States at 14,495 feet. There we exulted on that sparkling day at the wonderful panorama north, west, and south over the Sierra Nevadas, and east over the Mojave Desert. What a spot it is, with its pure air, turquoise lakes below, and vista giving way to vista as far as one could see—perhaps one hundred miles that day. As we gazed together from what seemed to be the top of the world, one student pointed out that only eighty miles to the southeast was Death Valley. This is the lowest spot in the United States at 280 feet below sea level and the hottest place in the country with a record 134 degrees in the shade.

What a contrast! One place is the top of the world—the other is the bottom. One place is perpetually cool—the other perpetually hot. From Mount Whitney you look down on all of life. From Death Valley you can only look up to the rest of the world. Some Californians travel to both places on the same day. It gives them something to brag about! But even more, this journey, from Death Valley to

Whitney's pinnacle in the heavens, enhances one's appreciation for the great contrasts in life.

We have something spiritually like this in the book of Ephesians where Paul purposely takes us down to the Death Valley of the soul (2:1–3), and then up to the soul's highest heaven "in the heavenly realms in Christ Jesus" (vv. 4–7). His method is contrast—from death to life; from hell to heaven; from bondage to freedom; from pessimism to optimism. This upward journey never fails to enhance our appreciation for what we have in Christ and influence the way we live.

## DEATH VALLEY

Paul begins at the very bottom of Death Valley. "As for you," he says, "you were dead in your transgressions and sins" (2:1). It is an absolute statement. He doesn't mean that the Ephesians were in danger of death before Christ, but that they were in a state of "real and present death."[1] Death here is not a figure of speech, but a fact. Paul means they were absolutely dead, in spirit. Moreover, though Paul says it of Gentiles, he includes his fellow Jews in verse 3—so that we understand that this state of spiritual death is universal. He is not describing some decadent, drugged-out segment of society, but all humanity from top to bottom. All people, regardless of their civilities and culture, are dead apart from Christ.

The bottom line here is: When Paul says "dead," he means it to have universal and absolute application, without exceptions. I have in my file a photograph of the corpse of the philosopher Jeremy Bentham, father of utilitarianism. The photo shows his body sitting in a chair dressed and hatted in proper early nineteenth century attire. The whole thing is the creation of Bentham's dark humor.

When he died he gave orders that his entire estate be

given to the University College Hospital in London on the condition that his body be preserved and placed in attendance at all the hospital's board meetings. This was duly carried out, and every year to this day Bentham is wheeled up to the board table and the chairman says: "Jeremy Bentham, present but not voting." It is, of course, a great joke on his utilitarianism. Jeremy Bentham will never raise his hand in response, nor will he ever submit a motion because he has been dead for over 150 years! The dead can do nothing. That is what Paul is talking to us about—the spiritual state of those apart from Christ.

How can this be? we may wonder, when unlike Jeremy Bentham, those without Christ are so very much alive. Their bodies are virile and robust; they have quick, active intellects and are brimming with personality. The answer is this: In the area that matters most, the soul, they have no life. Those who do not love Christ are blind to His reality, demands, and glory. Their souls are as deaf to the Holy Spirit as a corpse. "Abba, Father!" is not part of their vocabulary. Because of this, John Stott says: "We should not hesitate to reaffirm that a life without God (however physically fit and mentally alert the person may be) is a living death, and that those who live it are dead even while they are living."[2]

These are hard words. How does Paul support his thesis? The answer is that those who are spiritually dead are under the sway of the world, the devil, and the flesh, which is the order he names them in verses 2 and 3 of Ephesians.

## World

Regarding the domination of those without Christ by the world, Paul says in the first part of verse 2, "in which you used to live when you followed the ways of this world." The word for "world" (*kosmos*) is used 186 times in the Greek New Testament, and virtually every instance has an evil connotation. Corresponding with the word "ways" age means "the present evil age" (cf. Galatians 1:4). Those without Christ are captive to the social and value system of the present evil age that is alien and hostile to Christ. They are in willing captivity to culture. Today it is the pop culture of the media—the "group think" of the talk shows, post-Christian mores, and man-centered religious fads.

## Devil

Then there is the sway of the devil, whom Paul describes as "the ruler of the kingdom of the air, the spirit who is now at work in those who are disobedient" (v. 2). Satan is described in Scripture as "the prince of this world" (John 12:31), "the prince of demons" (Matthew 9:34), and by the sobering title "the god of this age" (2 Corinthians 4:4). As "ruler of the kingdom of the air" he commands innumerable hosts that operate in the unseen world and thus creates a general spirit of the age that energizes disobedience to God. We're talking about a sophisticated, high-tech Satan who drives culture. This is the devil's world in that sense, the *cosmos diabolicus* in which he knits just enough good with evil to achieve his purposes.

## Flesh

And, lastly, of course, is the flesh. "All of us also lived among them at one time, gratifying the cravings of our sinful nature [the flesh] and following its desires and thoughts. Like the rest, we were by nature objects of wrath" (v. 3). Our own fallen human nature leads us to cater to our desires and not God's will. Many of you will recall the joke about the girl who was disciplined by her mother for kicking her brother in the shins and then pulling his hair. "Sally, why did you let the devil make

you kick your little brother and pull his hair?"
Unabashedly Sally replies, "The devil made me kick him,
but pulling his hair was my idea!" There is no need for
the devil's influence—mankind sins very well on its own.

The spiritually dead are dominated by the world, the
devil, and the flesh. The world dominates from *without,*
the flesh from *within,* and the devil from *beyond*—the
terrible dynamics of spiritual death.

And with this, Paul concludes, "Like the rest, we were
by nature objects of wrath" (v. 3b). Everyone, Jews and
Gentiles, were, and are, sin-
ners "by nature"—they all
sinned in and with Adam and
are therefore guilty (Romans
5:12–14)—and are objects of
God's settled wrath. As the
apostle John said, "Whoever
believes in the Son has eternal life, but whoever rejects

> # DEAD MEN CANNOT RESPOND.

the Son will not see life, for God's wrath remains on him"
(John 3:36). Mankind is in the valley of death apart from
Christ.

It has been often noted that these verses in Ephesians
are a three-verse summary of the first three chapters of
the book of Romans, which teach the total depravity of
humankind. The biblical doctrine of depravity means
that every part of the human person is tainted by sin.[3] It
does not mean that all humans are equally depraved;
most do not go near the depths they could go. Nor does it
mean that humans are not capable of any good (cf. Luke
11:13). Nor does it mean that there is no dignity in man,
for there certainly is, as he is the imperfect bearer of the
divine image (Genesis 1:27).

No part of the human being (mind, emotions, heart,
will) is unaffected by the Fall. All of us are depraved,
completely. Because of this, apart from Christ, we are

totally lost. So profound is human depravity that near the end of his argument in Romans 3 Paul says, "There is no one righteous, not even one; there is no one who understands, no one who seeks God" (3:10–11). We often hear people say, "so-and-so is seeking after God." Indeed, it may be true if the Holy Spirit is prompting that person. But no man or woman does it on his or her own. They may be seeking the peace or status that salvation brings, but not God—if we are to believe His Word and not our sentiment. The biblical doctrine of depravity leads to the doctrine of man's spiritual death.

A former pastoral colleague of mine worked in a mortuary when he was in college and again in seminary. He told me that one night he walked into the darkened mortuary chapel and saw an open casket at the front of the chapel with a body lying in it. At this, he got down on his hands and knees and crept up silently to the casket, and then slowly elevated himself until he could see the tip of the man's nose and shouted, "Boo!" And you know what? The man didn't move an eyelash. The Jeremy Bentham principle is still in effect. Dead men cannot respond. In our state of spiritual death, we cannot respond to God's call to righteousness unless the Holy Spirit working within us motivates us.

The uniqueness of the biblical position concerning the human spirit can be seen when we note that in the long history of the human race there are (with variations) essentially three basic views of human nature: that man is well, that man is sick, and that man is dead. Supporters of the first view, that man is well, argue that all he needs is a good diet, exercise, and some vitamins. "I'm all right and you're all right" is his motto. Proponents of the second view agree that man is sick, maybe even mortally sick, but the situation is not hopeless, and that man will eventually cure himself. The biblical view is that man is neither well nor sick, but dead—"dead in [his] transgressions and sins"

(v. 1). All man's self-help will avail nothing![4] You can play reveille in the Arlington National Cemetery for a whole year and you will get no response from the dead.

Death Valley is where every soul resides who is outside Christ. It is a desolate image, almost exactly like the image Ezekiel gives in his thirty-seventh chapter:

> *"The hand of the LORD was upon me, and he brought me out by the Spirit of the LORD and set me in the middle of a valley; it was full of bones. He led me back and forth among them, and I saw a great many bones on the floor of the valley, bones that were very dry. He asked me, 'Son of man, can these bones live?' I said, 'O Sovereign LORD, you alone know.'" (Ezekiel 37:1–3)*

That everyone without Christ is dead is something that people don't want to hear today—and many are silent about the doctrine. But it is vitally important. Christ's death doesn't make any sense without it. Grace is incomprehensible without it. A short stay in Death Valley will make you aware of that fact, if you realize in time that that's where you are.

## THE HEIGHTS OF LIFE

### Resurrection!

The journey from Death Valley to the spiritual heights of life is nothing short of a resurrection. "But because of his great love for us, God, who is rich in mercy, made us alive with Christ even when we were dead in transgressions—it is by grace you have been saved" (Ephesians 2:4–5). The eminent New Testament scholar Marcus Barth says that "in the majority of occurrences in the New Testament, the verb 'to make alive' is a synonym of 'to raise' from the dead."[5] Man is dead, and only the radical path of resurrection can save him.

If you are truly a believer, you have experienced resurrection power. As Paul said earlier in 1:19–20, "That power is like the working of his mighty strength . . . when he raised him from the dead"—and you have known this power. We all are in one of two groups: those who are spiritually resurrected and those who are spiritually dead. Which are you? If you are "dead in your transgressions and sins," self-help is not going to do it. You cannot crawl from the casket. You must be "made . . . alive with Christ."

Christians, when you were dead in your transgressions, you were depraved in every area. There was nothing that sin did not taint. But if you have been made alive through the deep and genuine acknowledgment of Christ's resurrection, then His life touches every area. And, instead of "deprovement," there comes improvement. The archives of the Billy Graham Center contain the letter which the soon-to-be great evangelist Charles Fuller wrote to his wife the night of his conversion, July 16, 1916. "There has been a complete change in my life. Sunday I went up to Los Angeles and heard Paul Rader preach. I never heard such a sermon in all my life. Ephesians 1:18. Now my whole life and aims and ambitions are changed. I feel now that I want to serve God if he can use me instead of making the goal of life the making of money."[6] You too can have your whole life changed by understanding the power of Christ's resurrection. You can know the resurrection life and power, and experience it right now in your own life.

You can also come to see that you are the object of His love, mercy, and grace. See these words in verses 4 and 5. "But because of his great love for us, God, who is rich in mercy, made us alive with Christ even when we were dead in transgressions—it is by grace you have been saved." His love will transcend your depravity, His *mercy* will attend to your misery, and His *grace* will pardon your sin—and you will be "made alive with Christ."

### Ascension!

Then with your resurrection will come ascension to the heights of heaven. "And God raised us up with Christ and seated us with him in the heavenly realms in Christ Jesus" (v. 6). This is what life in Christ does for us in this life. Though

> # WE WERE IN DEATH VALLEY, IN DESOLATION, LOST, HOPELESS; BUT BY HIS RESURRECTION WE HAVE BEEN RAISED TO THE HIGHEST HEAVEN.

not yet physically there, you will spiritually be there seated with Christ by virtue of your union and incorporation in Christ. The powers of the spiritual realm will be brought to bear in your life now!

### Riches!

And what will be the end of all this? Actually, there will be no end, because as verse 7 concludes with His purpose, *"in order that in the coming ages he might show the incomparable riches of his grace, expressed in his kindness to us in Christ Jesus."* A Roman matron was once asked, "Where are your jewels?" She responded by calling her two sons, and, pointing to them, said, "These are my jewels."[7] So it is with Christ and us. He is going to show the all-surpassing riches of His grace to us in the "limitless future, as age succeeds age."[8] There is nothing static here. He will show His grace and kindness before His return, at His return, after His return, and in all ages.[9] It will keep unfolding into the ages of the ages, on and on and on!

On that beautiful day as we stood on the pinnacle of Mount Whitney rejoicing at its beauty, a Navy jet buzzed us, breaking the sound barrier as it crossed the summit about one hundred feet over our heads. Then he did barrel rolls off into the horizon, only to come back the opposite direction and do the same thing. He was having a good time, but his thrill didn't compare to ours! He was just an observer—passing by in a bubble. We were there—standing on the summit breathing alpine freshness, feeling God's creation. There is only one thing that would have made it better—and that is rising from Death Valley that morning—from the lowest to the highest.

But we have done it in Christ. We were all in Death Valley, in desolation, lost, hopeless; but by His resurrection we have been raised to the highest heaven! We are fully alive.

Where are you right now? "Dead in your transgressions and sins"? Or "made alive with Christ"? If you are without life, there is resurrection power available for you, even if you are as the parched bones of Death Valley.

*The hand of the LORD was upon me, and he brought me out by the Spirit of the LORD and set me in the middle of a valley; it was full of bones. He led me back and forth among them, and I saw a great many bones on the floor of the valley, bones that were very dry. He asked me, "Son of man, can these bones live?" I said, "O Sovereign LORD, you alone know." Then he said to me, "Prophesy to these bones and say to them, 'Dry bones, hear the word of the LORD! This is what the Sovereign LORD*

*says to these bones: I will make breath enter you,
and you will come to life. I will attach tendons to
you and make flesh come upon you and cover you
with skin; I will put breath in you, and you will
come to life. Then you will know that I am the
LORD.'" So I prophesied as I was commanded. And
as I was prophesying, there was a noise, a rattling
sound, and the bones came together, bone to bone.
I looked, and tendons and flesh appeared on them
and skin covered them, but there was no breath in
them. Then he said to me, "Prophesy to the breath;
prophesy, son of man, and say to it, 'This is what
the Sovereign LORD says:*

*Come from the four winds, O breath, and breathe
into these slain, that they may live.' "So I
prophesied as he commanded me, and breath
entered them; they came to life and stood up on
their feet—a vast army."
(Ezekiel 37:1–10)*

If you realize that you are dead in your transgressions and sins and an object of wrath, desperately in need of God's grace, and that you can do nothing to save yourself—you are in the way of grace. Simply cast yourself on Jesus, asking Him to take away your sins and give you life—and He will breathe life into you and set you alongside Him in the heavenly places. Are you ready? If so, ask Him now. If not, the next chapter will be of further help.

# NOTES

1. T. H. L. Parker, trans., *The Epistles of Paul the Apostle to the Galatians, Ephesians, Philippians and Colossians*, Vol. 11 of Calvin's Commentaries, (Grand Rapids: Eerdmans, 1974), 139.

2. John R. W. Stott, *God's New Society: The Message of Ephesians* (Downers Grove, IL: InterVarsity, 1979), 72.

3. See also, Ford Lewis Battles, *Calvin: Institutes of the Christian Religion*, Vol. 2 (Philadelphia: Westminster, 1975), 251 who says: "Original sin, therefore, seems to be a hereditary depravity and corruption of our nature, diffused into all parts of the soul, which first makes us liable to God's wrath, then also brings forth in us those works which Scripture calls 'works of the flesh' (Gal. 5:19)."

4. James Montgomery Boice, *Foundations of the Christian Faith* (Downers Grove, IL: InterVarsity, 1986), 200–201.

5. Marcus Barth, *Ephesians Introduction, Translation, and Commentary on Chapters 1–3* (Garden City, NY: Doubleday, 1974), 219–20.

6. *Illustration Cornucopia*, Summer, 1984, Number 1, Archives of the Billy Graham Center, Wheaton College, Wheaton, IL.

7. William Hendriksen, *Exposition of Ephesians* (Grand Rapids: Baker, 1970), 119.

8. F. F. Bruce, *The Epistle to the Ephesians* (London: Pickering & Inglis Ltd., 1973), 51.

9. Hendriksen, *Exposition of Ephesians* pp. 119–20.

## FOR FURTHER REFERENCE

1. List as many effects as you can of being spiritually dead.

2. Why is it a grace to understand that you are dead in your sins?

3. What does *depravity* mean? And what does it not mean?

4. What does Christ's resurrection mean to us? What special power does it hold for us to become spiritually alive?

5. If you haven't been made alive in Christ (because you are dead in your sins), are you willing now to ask Him to take away your sins and give you life?

# *grace*
# THROUGH FAITH

G reek mythology tells the story of the mortal Sisyphus, a violent thug who waylaid travelers for their wealth and then murdered them. He also betrayed the secrets of the gods and was responsible for chaining the god of death, Thanatos, so that he couldn't help the dead reach the underworld, leaving them to wander aimlessly. For his transgressions, the god Hades condemned him for eternity to roll a large boulder up a tall hill. Each time he reached the top, the boulder would roll back down and he would be forced to repeat the process, again and again and again.

Unfortunately for some people, trying to earn a ticket into heaven through acts of good works is like rolling Sisyphus's boulder up that hill—they'll never stay at the top. A popular survey taken a few years ago asked people who they thought most likely to get into heaven. Oprah Winfrey and Michael Jordan topped the list with 67 percent and 66 percent approval ratings respectively. Popular though these people may be, God's plan for salvation doesn't work by consensus either. These approval ratings are nonworking numbers as far as reaching God's kingdom is concerned. So are the number of good deeds we do. Fortunately for us, God has a better plan, as we will see.

So how then are we saved? First, we answer with Paul's negative affirmation in verse 9 of Ephesians 2: "not by works, so that no one can boast." It is absolutely essential that you understand this, and believe this, if you are to be saved. Salvation does not come by works.

If you accept the Bible's teaching that salvation is "not by works," you will be going against the notions and direction of our culture. An unbelieving preacher illustrated his philosophy by telling of a frog which fell into a large milk can. Try as it would, it couldn't get out of the milk. It paddled and paddled but to no apparent avail. There was nothing to do but keep paddling, which it did, until it churned a pad of butter, and presto!—it was able to jump out of the milk and was saved! "Just keep your chin up folks, be positive, and paddle like heck and you'll make it!"

If I fell into a pail of milk I would keep paddling as long as I could, but I wouldn't make that my philosophy of achieving eternal salvation. To think like that is to fall into the ancient Pelagian heresy that Saint Augustine fought so passionately to defeat. But the sad truth is, the frog is an apt symbol of American folk religion. "Just keep on keeping on and you'll be all right"—"I'm a good person, not perfect, but there are a whole lot of people worse than I"—"God knows I'm not perfect, but I'm doing my best." That's OK talk for Kermit the frog, but it's not the language of salvation!

The reasons salvation is not by works are several. Our text gives us one, which is—"so that no one can boast." It's certain that if salvation came by works, eternity would spawn a fraternity of chest-thumping boasters—an endless line of celestial Muhammad Alis shouting, "I'm the greatest!" or even worse, Pharisees— "God, I thank you that I am not like other men—robbers, evildoers, adulterers" (Luke 18:11).

Jesus substantiates that this is what heaven would be like if salvation came by works in His parable of the sheep and the goats in Matthew 25. The goats on His *left* do all the boasting, and are sent to judgment (Matthew 25:44; cf. 7–22); the sheep on His *right* (the saved who go on to their heavenly reward) cannot even recall their good deeds (Matthew 25:37–39; cf. 40–46), for *salvation does not come by works.* No one who is saved will have grounds to boast before God—or even want to.

But as true as this is, there are even deeper reasons that salvation is not by works, namely, the utter sinfulness of humanity contrasted with God's transcending standard of righteousness. God is radically righteous (Romans 1:17; 3:21). He is righteousness, and no human can attain His standard because we are radically sinful beings. The word *radical* comes from the Latin word *radix,* which means root. Thus, the very root of our being is sinful. This is why every part of our person is tainted with sin. This is behind the apostle Paul's devastating litany of condemnation in Romans 3:10–18. Here he employs the rabbinical technique of *charaz* (Hebrew for string of pearls) in stringing together an overwhelming list of evidences which prove the universally corrupt *character* (vv. 10–12) and *conduct* (vv. 13–18) of all men. Therefore, even our very best works are colored by sin— so that they never come near approaching the radical righteousness that God demands. No matter how high we climb our moral ladder, it is not high enough. This is why Paul says that salvation is "not by works."

All our paddling in the butter churn will not do it. Imagine an airplane flying over the South Atlantic and suddenly crashing a thousand miles from any coast. In the plane there are three individuals who, for the sake of comic relief and familiarity, we shall identify as Kermit, Bert, and Big Bird. Kermit (the frog) is a great Olympic

> # THE LOVE OF GOD IS GOING OUT TOWARD THE UTTERLY UNDESERVING.

swimmer, Bert is an average swimmer, and, lastly, Big Bird cannot swim at all. Kermit calls out from the sinking plane, "Follow me, I'll get you out of this! *Comprende?*"—and he takes off with an impressive crawl heading for the tip of South America a thousand miles away. The other two jump after him. Quickly Big Bird goes down to Davy Jones's Locker. It takes about thirty minutes for Bert the swimmer to be deep-sixed. But Kermit churns away for twenty-five hours. He has covered fifty miles. An amazing feat! Only 475 more hours to go! He'll be there in nineteen days if he doesn't slow down. Needless to say, Kermit doesn't make it either.

The truth is, despite our popular folk religion, our paddling will never do, no matter how good we are. The distance is too far and we are too flawed. We can try, but all our works will be no more beneficial than rearranging the deck chairs on the Titanic, giving us a better view as we go down. The Bible says, "not by works"—but the question is, do we believe it?

Suppose I went to my best friend and said, "Jack, you are a terrific person, but I don't believe a thing you say." How would he feel? This is the way some people treat God. "God, I believe You are great. I believe that Jesus is real. I simply can't believe Your Word that it's *not by works.*"

We don't have that option. He didn't leave it to us. Do you see that salvation is not by works? Most importantly, do you truly believe it? If so, you're right at the door, for

Jesus says, "Blessed are those who realize that they have nothing within themselves to commend them to God, for theirs is the kingdom of heaven" (my paraphrase of Matthew 5:3).

## BY GRACE

If our good works cannot save us, then how are we saved? The answer from the Bible is *by grace*, "For it is by grace you have been saved, through faith—and this not from yourselves, it is the gift of God" (Ephesians 2:8).

Grace? It is unmerited favor—the love of God going out toward the utterly undeserving. It has reference here to the forgiveness of sin, and then the riches that Christ brings. It is a lavish, sumptuous, joyous word. But the great and transcending emphasis of our text is that it is a free gift, totally gratuitous. Where our text says, *"and this not from yourselves,"* the idea is, *"By God's grace you are people who have been saved through faith, and this whole event and experience is . . . God's free gift to you."*[1]

A large prestigious church had three mission churches under its care. On the first Sunday of the New Year all the members of the mission churches came to the big city church for a combined Communion service. In those mission churches, which were located in the slums of the city, were some outstanding cases of conversions—thieves, burglars, and so on—but all knelt side by side at the Communion rail.

On one such occasion the pastor saw a former burglar kneeling beside a judge of the Supreme Court of England—the very judge who had sent him to jail where he had served seven years. After his release this burglar had been converted and become a Christian worker. Yet, as they knelt there, the judge and the former convict, neither one seemed to be aware of the other.

After the service, the judge was walking out with the pastor and said to him, "Did you notice who was kneeling beside me at the Communion rail this morning?" The pastor replied, "Yes, but I didn't know that you noticed." The two walked along in silence for a few more moments, and then the judge said, "What a miracle of grace." The pastor nodded in agreement. "Yes, what a marvelous miracle of grace." Then the judge said, "But to whom do you refer?" And the pastor said, "Why, to the conversion of that convict." The judge said, "But I was not referring to him. I was thinking of myself." The pastor, surprised, replied, "You were thinking of yourself? I don't understand." "Yes," the judge replied, "it was natural for the burglar to receive God's grace when he came out of jail. He had nothing but a history of crime behind him, and when he saw Jesus as his Savior he knew there was salvation and hope and joy for him. And he knew how much he needed that help. But look at me. I was taught from earliest infancy to live as a gentleman; that my word was to be my bond; that I was to say my prayers, to go to church, take Communion and so on. I went through Oxford, took my degrees, was called to the bar and eventually became a judge. Pastor, it was God's grace that drew me; it was God's grace that opened my heart to receive it. I'm a greater miracle of His grace."

Perhaps there is something to the judge's insistence upon his life being the greater miracle. But, in either case, it was God's free, unearned grace, and certainly not works that brought salvation.

Again, how contrary to the spirit of the age this is—especially American culture—"We make our money the old-fashioned way. We earn it!" And for this I applaud John Houseman—if it's true. Such a mentality is proper in its realm. But in regard to salvation it is lethal. "For it is by grace you have been saved, through faith—and this not from yourselves, it is the gift of God" (v. 8). It is all of grace. Paul reinforces this in Romans 11:6, "And if by grace, then it is no longer by works; if it were, grace would no longer be grace." The fact is, as soon as there is a mixture of even the smallest percentage of works, grace is debased and perverted. Salvation is by grace alone. No one will be saved except through God's unmerited, unearned grace. Do you believe it?

Pascal said, "Grace is indeed required to turn a man into a saint; and he who doubts this does not know what either a man or a saint is"[2] and he is so "right on"—for the doubter does not understand how

> *No ear may hear His coming,*
> *But in this world of sin,*
> *Where meek souls will receive Him still*
> *The dear Christ enters in.*
>                                      —Philip Brooks, 1868

It's Christmas every day for the humble. Are you meek enough to receive His grace?—to admit you can't do it? If so, you must listen with all you have to Paul's third point—which is that salvation comes "through faith."

## THROUGH FAITH

*For it is by grace you have been saved, through faith—and this not from yourselves, it is the gift of God. (v. 8)*

If there is no faith there is no grace—and no salvation. In Scripture faith/belief is the thing that God honors more than any single thing.

*Believe* in the Lord Jesus, and you will be saved.
*(Acts 16:31, emphasis mine)*

*Yet to all who received him, to those who* **believed**
*in his name, he gave the right to become children*
*of God. (John 1:12, emphasis mine)*

*Through him everyone who* **believes** *is justified*
*from everything you could not be justified from by*
*the law of Moses. (Acts 13:39, emphasis mine)*

*to the man who does not work but* **trusts** *God who*
*justifies the wicked, his faith is credited as*
*righteousness. (Romans 4:5, emphasis mine)*

No one has sins forgiven, no one goes to heaven, no
one has peace until there is faith in Jesus Christ.

What then is faith? Faith is not the mere intellectual
reception of Christian truth, nor is it belief alone. Faith
is belief, but belief is not faith. *True faith is belief plus
trust.* How is this?

There is a story from the last century which can help.
During the 1800s there was a famous acrobat known all
over the world. His name was Jean Francois Gravelet,
better known by his stage name, Blondin. Born in France
in 1824, Blondin became well known while still a child.

As he grew older his skill and showmanship brought
him fame throughout Europe and America. Once in London he played the violin on a tightrope 170 feet off the
ground—and then did a somersault wearing stilts. His
most spectacular feats were the crossings of Niagara
Falls on a tightrope, 1,100 feet long and 160 feet above
the water. On one occasion he took a stove onto the
tightrope and cooked an omelet over the roaring falls.
*"Bon appetit!"* On another occasion he pushed a wheel-
barrow across blindfolded. On still another, he stood on

his head over the falls. That is why today in London there are Niagara and Blondin Avenues.

Once, in an unusual demonstration of skill, Blondin carried a man across Niagara Falls on his back. After putting his rider down, he turned to the large crowd and asked a man close by, "Do you believe I could do that with you?" "Of course," the man answered, "I've just seen you do it." "Hop on," said Blondin, "I'll carry you across." "Not on your life!" the man called back. Just so! *There is no real faith without trust!*

To be truthful, I would never have hopped on Blondin either. In fact, I wouldn't do it between my front door and the street, if the rope were more than ten feet off the ground. The reasons are three: First there is the *me factor.* What if I "lost it"? Down we would go. Then there is the *chance factor.* What if the rope broke? Finally there is the *Blondin factor.* What if the only time he makes a mistake in his whole life is with me? Don't get me wrong, I *believe* with all my heart he could do it, but I just don't *trust* him with my life!

# YOU CANNOT MIX WORKS AND GRACE IN RESPECT TO ETERNAL SALVATION.

But it's a universe of difference between the tightrope walker and Jesus! He can't drop me. I can't even drop myself. And there is no such thing as chance. Do you *believe* that Jesus is who He says He is? Do you *believe* that He died for your sins? Do you *believe* He was resurrected and lives today? Have you *trusted* Him to save you? Have you accepted His invitation?

The only way from the Death Valley of the soul to the

highest heavens of spiritual life is to be carried there by Jesus. And for this to happen there are some things you must understand and believe—for they are the Gospel in a nutshell.

Understand first that salvation is not "by works." Do you believe that what the Bible says is true? Do you see that your best will never get you there because you are radically sinful and God is radically righteous? Do you see that your works are nothing more than rearranging the chairs on a sinking ship—a frog paddling in a sea of infinity? If so, you're right at the door.

Then, you must see and believe that salvation is only "by grace"—a completely free gift. *"For it is by grace you have been saved, through faith—and this not from your-selves, it is the gift of God"* (Ephesians 2:8). You must understand and believe that you cannot mix works and grace in respect to eternal salvation. Are you humble enough to say, "Not by works that I have done, but humbly to the Cross I come. God, if I'm going to be saved, it is by your grace and nothing else"?

> *Where meek souls will receive Him still*
> *The dear Christ enters in.*
> —Phillip Brooks, 1868

Finally, you must *understand* and *believe* that it is "through faith"—and *trust* Him alone for your salvation. Have you stepped out onto Jesus and received the gift of eternal life? Can you trust Him now? The Bible says, *"Believe in the Lord Jesus, and you will be saved"* (Acts 16:31). Are you trusting Him alone? Then welcome!

# NOTES

1. John R. W. Stott, *God's New Society: The Message of Ephesians* (Downers Grove, IL: InterVarsity, 1979), 83. See also *Calvin, Commentary:* "He does not mean that faith is the gift of God, but that salvation is given to us by God, or, that we obtain it by the gift of God," 145. Also, Bruce: "It is the whole concept of salvation by grace through faith that is descended as the gift of God," 51.
2. W. H. Auden and Louis Kronenberger, *The Viking Book of Aphorisms* (New York: Dorset, 1966), 89.

## FOR FURTHER REFERENCE

1. Who around you do you think will enter the kingdom of God? Why? List your reasons for three people you know well.

2. Why do many "good" people reject the teaching of salvation of Ephesians 2:8–9?

3. How do verses 1–3 support Paul's contention in verses 8–9 that salvation does not come by works?

4. Why does God's saving grace require a humble heart?

5. Saving faith is more than mental. It requires belief plus trust. How does the story of Blondin illustrate this?

6. Why must faith be a gift of God?

7. Are you trusting Christ alone for your salvation?

# *not far from*
# THE KINGDOM

*One of the teachers of the law came and heard them debating. Noticing that Jesus had given them a good answer, he asked him, "Of all the commandments, which is the most important?"*

*"The most important one," answered Jesus, "is this: 'Hear, O Israel, the Lord our God, the Lord is one. Love the Lord your God with all your heart and with all your soul and with all your strength.' The second is this: 'Love your neighbor as yourself.' There is no commandment greater than these."*

*"Well said, teacher," the man replied. "You are right in saying that God is one and there is no other but him. To love him with all your heart, with all your understanding and with all your strength, and to love your neighbor as yourself is more important than all burnt offerings and sacrifices."*

*When Jesus saw that he had answered wisely, he said to him, "You are not far from the kingdom of God." (Mark 12:28–34)*

Few people have so affected history that its very epochs are marked by their births—let alone their spiritual rebirths! John Wesley was one of the few. Had it not been for Wesley's conversion and the ensuing revival with its social impact, England would probably have undergone something similar to the French Revolution. John Wesley's coming to faith was one of the most important historical events in the Western world.

John Wesley was born in 1703, the fifteenth child of Samuel Wesley, the rector of Epworth, and his wife, Susanna. He enjoyed a good upbringing under his unusually talented and dedicated mother. He had a brilliant career at Charterhouse and Oxford, where he was elected fellow of Lincoln College in 1726. After serving as his father's assistant on two occasions, he was ordained a priest in the Church of England in 1728.

Returning to Oxford, Wesley joined a group of undergraduates led by his brother, Charles, and the later-to-be great evangelist, George Whitefield. This group, which was dedicated to building a holy life, was derisively nicknamed by other Oxonians the "Holy Club." Though Wesley was not yet truly converted, he met with these men for prayer, the study of the Greek New Testament, and devotional exercises.

He set aside an hour each day for private prayer and reflection. He took Communion each week, and resolved to conquer every sin. He fasted twice a week, visited the prisons, and assisted the poor and the sick. Doing all this helped him imagine he was a Christian.

In 1735, still unconverted, he accepted an invitation from the Society for the Propagation of the Gospel to become a missionary to the American Indians in Georgia. His ministry was a great fiasco. He utterly failed as a missionary—undergoing miserable conflicts with his colleagues, and almost dying of disease. When he returned to England, he wrote: "I went to America to convert the Indians; but, oh, who shall convert me?" His mission experience taught him the wickedness and waywardness of his own heart.

Not all, however, was lost. In his travels aboard ship he met some German Moravian Christians whose simple faith made a great impression on him. When he returned to London, he sought out one of their leaders. Through a series of conversations, to quote Wesley's own words, he was "clearly convinced of unbelief, of the want of that faith whereby alone we are saved."

Then on the morning of May 24, 1738, something happened that Wesley could never forget. He opened his Bible and his eyes fell on the text of Mark 12:34: "You are not far from the kingdom of God." The words reassured him. Before he went to bed that night, he crossed that invisible line into the kingdom of God. This text was to become Wesley's life verse, a reminder of the shape of his life for the first thirty-five years of his existence. "You are not far from the kingdom of God."

Beautifully, not only the verse, but its setting (the Lord is conversing with a scribe, a lost clergyman of the house of Israel), bears remarkable parallels to Wesley's own lostness. Both were clergymen. Both were highly educated. Both were Bible scholars who knew the Bible inside and out. Both were confronted with Christ, who said to both, "You are not far from the kingdom of God."

## NEAR THE KINGDOM OF GOD

The exchange, of which our text is a part, began with a question from the scribe: "One of the teachers of the law came and heard them debating. Noticing that Jesus had given them a good answer, he asked him, 'Of all the commandments, which is the most important?'" (v. 28). The scribe initially had come to witness the confrontation between Jesus and the Sadducees. Though he disliked the Sadducees' doctrine, he came to cheer them on because they, like he, had a religion of human achievement. Jesus was a threat to his belief system. However, as he witnessed the breathtaking intelligence of Jesus in answering the resurrection question, refuting the Sadducees with a quotation from Exodus 3:6 (from the very heart of the Torah), he found himself inwardly applauding Jesus and subconsciously drawn to Him. Before he knew it, he was impulsively asking a question, and his was his own question. It came from the scribal mind game of trying to reduce religion to a single axiom. Rabbi Hillel, for example, was promised by a Gentile that he would convert if Hillel could give him the whole Law while he stood on one foot. Hillel answered with a version of the Golden Rule: "What you yourself hate, do not do to your neighbor; this is the whole Law—the rest is commentary. Go and learn it!"[1] This is the kind of answer the scribe was looking for from Jesus. He was standing heart-to-heart with eternity.

The scribe was not to be disappointed, for Jesus' reply was consummately brilliant: "The most important one," answered Jesus, "is this: 'Hear, O Israel, the Lord our God, the Lord is one. Love the Lord your God with all your heart and with all your soul and with all your mind and with all your strength.' The second is this: 'Love your neighbor as yourself.' There is no commandment greater than these" (vv. 29–31).

The first part of Jesus' answer was known to everyone. It is from the *Shema Israel*, "Hear, O Israel," the opening sentence of every synagogue worship service, taken from Deuteronomy 6:4. It was repeated by every pious Jew every morning and every evening. In fact, it was worn by the devout in a tiny leather box, called a phylactery, on the forehead and on the wrist during prayer. Godly households also hung the Shema on their doors in a small round box called a mezuzah. Everyone knew this part of Jesus' answer. It was the creed of Israel. Heart, soul, mind, and strength were not intended as a breakdown or a psychological analysis of human personality.

They simply meant that one's whole being is to be devoted to loving God. It does not take much of a man to be a believer, but it takes all of him there is.

The second part of Jesus' answer is taken from Leviticus 19:18, "love your neighbor as yourself." This also was familiar to all Jews. So where was the genius in Jesus' answer? It was in this: The thought of loving God and loving humankind had been voiced by other rabbis and scribes, but this was the first time any rabbi had fused these two specific Scripture references together.[2]

> **SOME PEOPLE ARE FAR FROM THE KINGDOM OF GOD, SOME ARE AT THE THRESHOLD.**

The brilliance of Jesus' answer lay not only in its formulation but in its implications. First, it summarizes the first four commandments, which have to do with our love for God (Exodus 20:2–11). The second part summarizes the final six commandments, which have to do with our love for humankind (Exodus 20:12–17). Jesus' answer is comprehensive to the "nth degree."

Second, Jesus' double answer shows that love for God and love for humankind cannot be divided. This teaching had a powerful impact on the subsequent teaching of the apostolic church. Later the apostle John wrote, "Whoever loves God must also love his brother" (1 John 4:21; cf. Romans 13:8–9; Galations 5:14; James 2:8).

Third, Jesus' command to love your neighbor "as yourself" radicalizes the call to human love. None of the earlier formulations included this qualifying clause. Including

"as yourself" provides us with a conscious and con-
science-convicting standard, because we sinners all love
ourselves, despite our psychological demurrals. Just how
radical Jesus' demand is can be seen in the story of the
Good Samaritan, where he portrayed a neighbor not as
a fellow Jew, as any Jew would have expected, but as an
enemy, a Gentile—from the world next door (Luke
10:25–27).

What powerful teaching this was! This marvelous
symmetry of devotion—loving God and loving humankind
—could not be disputed. Nobody had ever put it so well,
or so scripturally, until now! It was brilliant! It was perfect! It truly encompassed the whole Law. And the obvious ethos of Christ's own person (He was living it) made
it so compelling.

How would the scribe answer? Remember, his
cronies were standing by, watching. The New Testament
scholar C. E. B. Cranfield says that the opening words in
verse 32, which our text in Mark 12 renders, "Well said,"
should really be an exclamation[3]—perhaps "Beautifully
said, teacher! What a beautiful answer!" The scribe told
Jesus, "You are right in saying that God is one and there
is no other but him. To love him with all your heart,
with all your understanding and with all your strength,
and to love your neighbor as yourself is more important
than all burnt offerings and sacrifices" (vv. 32, 33). Our
Lord was clearly pleased with his response: "When Jesus
saw that he had answered wisely, he said to him, 'You
are not far from the kingdom of God'" (v. 34). Jesus'
answer was tantalizingly ambiguous. He was after the
scribe's soul.

This was a *compliment*. From the scribe's response,
Jesus saw that the man was capable of thinking for himself. He saw that the scribe understood that the Law was
more than a system, that is was essentially spiritual. So
He complimented him: "The way you're thinking, you're

not very far from the kingdom of God." Some people are far from the kingdom of God, some at the threshold. The scribe was very close.

This was also a *warning*. Though he was close, he was decisively separated. It is possible to be within an inch of heaven yet go to hell!

Here Jesus' point was positive: The man was near! How so? He realized that loving God and humankind "is more important than all burnt offerings and sacrifices." This tells us much about his heart, because he speaks of the entire ceremonial system as not being as important as loving God. What he was saying was light-years beyond the place at which many people have arrived today who imagine that their good works will suffice. The scribe was near!

The scribe was also a thinking man. Jesus complimented him for this by telling him that he had "answered wisely." He was intellectually convinced that Christ was right. Samuel Johnson said: "If a man thinks deeply, he thinks religiously." In a world that is about as shallow as a birdbath, those who enter the kingdom are those who are willing to pause and truly think about eternal things.

The scribe was also near because he faced head-on the implications of the fact that the love of God is the highest priority of all. Squarely faced, this is a sobering reality, because by nature we do not love God with all our heart, no matter how hard we try. There has to be a radical change inside us in order for us to do this. This is a work of the Spirit of God. By embracing the necessity of love the scribe drew near to heaven's door.

He was also near because he was honest. He was a scribe, and naturally sided with his fellow scribes and Pharisees. But he did not let his natural allegiance keep him from acknowledging the truth. There is always hope for a person who will break ranks to keep his or her conscience. The scribe was nearer than most.

He was also near because he was not a coward. He was willing to risk mocking in order to step up to the door of the kingdom of God. Lack of courage and love of approval have been fatal to many souls. This man was so near to the kingdom—so near!

John Wesley was like that. Sitting at the feet of one of England's most famous mothers, he was taught that the love of God was the highest priority of all. Susanna Wesley's own testimony was that she spent regular time with each of her nineteen children, instructing them in the things of God.

Wesley was a thinking man if there ever was one! He was famous for his unadorned clarity in a day of ornamental obfuscation. He brought all his intelligence to bear on eternal things. After his experience in America, he bared his soul without guile to those he thought could help him. Wesley was also brave and refused to be a "people-pleaser."

With all of this he was so near, but still not in the kingdom. His biggest problem was understanding the inward nature of Christ's requirements.

Wesley was a master of external discipline (fastings, prayers, and good deeds). Yet, as he later explained, after he stood in the face of death his religious exercise gave him little comfort, and no assurance of his acceptance by God.

## FAR FROM THE KINGDOM

If we are to believe God's Word first and then the testimony of John Wesley as well, we must take to heart this truth: While the scribe and his clerical counterpart, John Wesley, were not far from the kingdom, they were still outside. Being almost there is not being there!

Perhaps you recall some years ago that stuntman Evel Knievel tried to jump the Snake River in his jet-motorcycle. He went up with a burst of power, then fizzled out across the canyon, ignominiously pulling the ripcord of his parachute. Making it halfway, or even all but an inch, is not making it.

Today, in some circles, it is fashionable to talk about "spiritual pilgrimages." That is OK in the context of a regenerated life. We are certainly part of a growing experience. However, if the word "pilgrimage" is used to sanctify or baptize the state of not arriving at something good, it is a deception. Being on a pilgrimage can sound so humble. It implies that you do not have the proud audacity to say you have arrived. It means that you are not an "absolutist"—something akin to a fascist or racist in the relativistic thinking of the world. But being a pilgrim must not be an end in itself. You must make it into the kingdom or your pilgrimage is of no use at all.

Did the scribe ever make it into the kingdom? We do not know. The Scriptures are silent.

## GETTING INTO THE KINGDOM

If the scribe finally did enter the kingdom of heaven it was because he submitted to the logic of his own words. Loving God is more important than the entire ceremonial system. Perhaps he attempted to love God with all his heart and failed, thus realizing that he could never achieve the moral excellency of the Law and that he was a lost sinner. Finally seeing himself for what he was, he may have cast himself on the mercy of God, and thus found salvation.

When a religious man sees and acknowledges the profundity of his sin, it is a great day. Sir James Y. Simpson, the discoverer of chloroform, used to say that the greatest discovery he ever made was that he was a sinner and that Jesus Christ was the Savior he needed. Such a discovery will lead to the casting of yourself on the mercy of God, and thus receiving the gift of faith, repentance, and salvation.

This is what happened to Wesley. His experience in America had brought him to the end of himself. His honest interchange with the Moravians who witnessed to him brought further conviction of his inner failure. On one occasion as he talked with them, he heard them speak of their personal faith as a gift from God. When he asked how this could be, they replied that this faith was the free gift of God. They assured him that God would unfailingly give it to everyone who earnestly and perseveringly sought it. Wesley wrote after the meeting that he resolved to seek it to the end.

> # CONVICTIONS NOT ACTED ON DIE.

Finally, on May 24, 1738, as Wesley opened his Bible, he read that beautiful statement that in nine words condensed the progress of his spiritual pilgrimage: "You are not far from the kingdom of God." Then came evening, and the famous statement in his journal tells the story. "In the evening I went very unwillingly to a society in Aldersgate Street where one was reading Luther's preface to the Epistle to the Romans. About a quarter before nine, while he was describing the change which God works in the heart through faith in Christ, I felt my heart strangely warmed. I felt I did trust in Christ, *Christ alone*, for salvation; and an assurance was given me, that He had taken away my sins, *even mine*, and saved me from the law of sin and death."[4]

The rest of the story is well-known in history. Wesley became a dreamer. He preached in Saint Mary's in Oxford. He preached in other churches. He preached in the mines. He preached in the fields. He preached on the streets. He preached on horseback. He even preached on his father's tombstone. *John Wesley didn't tire!* John Wesley preached 42,000 sermons. He averaged 4,500 miles a year. He rode sixty to seventy miles a day and preached three sermons a day on an average. When he was eighty-three, he wrote in his diary, "I am a wonder to myself. I am never tired, either with preaching, writing, or travelling!"[5]

As we all know, the church has never been the same. Wesley's disciples, including Francis Asbury, were mighty powers in evangelizing England and frontier America. Read his life and the lives of his circuit riders and you will find chronicled the most amazing love for Christ and a tenacious love for lost souls. Their lives are among the great glories of the Church Universal.

What are the lessons for us? First, it is entirely possible to have grown up in the church, to have consistent, godly parents, and yet never have come to a saving knowledge of Christ.

Second, it is also completely possible to have studied theology and have never become a true Christian. One can know the Scriptures in the original, as Wesley did, and know more than the preacher, yet be unregenerate still.

Third, it is possible to have heard the grace of Christ preached all your life and still be resting on your own goodness.

Fourth, it is possible to become Gospel-hardened, and so seal your damnation even within the church. It is possible to fool everyone and have the preacher conduct your funeral and assure everyone that your soul is resting in heaven—when it really is in hell.

Fifth, it is possible to be within just an inch of the kingdom of God.

The abiding truth is this: Convictions not acted on die; truths not followed fade; lingering can become a habit; and we can either go in or go farther away.[6]

Are you near to the kingdom of God, but not in?
There are times when a single step makes all the difference. When a man or woman stands at the entrance to
an airplane, one step and the person is on the way to a
new destination. But one who fails to act will never go
anywhere.

# NOTES

1. William L. Lane, *The Gospel According to Mark* (Grand Rapids: Eerdmans, 1975), 432.
2. William Barclay, *The Gospel of Mark* (Philadelphia: Westminster, 1956), 309.
3. C. E. B. Cranfield, *The Gospel According to St. Mark* (Cambridge: Cambridge University Press, 1983), 379.
4. James McGraw, *Great Evangelical Preachers of Yesterday* (Nashville: Abingdon, 1961), 57.
5. Cited in William Barclay, *The Letters to the Corinthians* (Philadelphia: Westminster, 1956), 289.
6. Alexander Maclaren, *Expositions of Holy Scripture, Vol. 8* (Grand Rapids: Baker, 1975), 150.

# CONCLUSION

Over the course of these chapters there have been numerous calls to believe and receive the matchless grace of Christ. Still, you may not have responded. It is possible to be near the kingdom and remain an eternity away.

The Scriptures warn us that "now is the day of salvation" (2 Corinthians 6:2). And "Today, if you hear his voice, do not harden your hearts" (Hebrews 3:7; cf. Psalm 95:7–8). This is the time to settle matters once for all.

## 1 PETER 2:24

Because of God's marvelous grace, there is only one "work" for you to do—and that is to *believe* (John 6:29). And here I can think of no more helpful text than 1 Peter 2:24. This is because at memorable times during my forty years of ministry I have asked inquirers to read the verse inserting their own names for the personal pronouns. Often they have believed in the process. Sometimes tears have fallen on this verse.

Will you prayerfully do this now by inserting your name? Find a quiet place. Quiet your heart. Now ask

God to open your eyes and give you the grace to believe as you slowly read:

**He himself bore _____'s sins in his own body on the tree, so that _____ might die to sins and live for righteousness. By his wounds _____has been healed.**

Did Jesus bear your sins on the Cross? If so, where are they now? Do you truly believe this? Are you resting all your hope on Him alone? If the answer is "yes," welcome to the kingdom!

Now, you must tell your Christian friends. Why not pick up the phone right now? You need the fellowship of a good church where the Bible is taught. And you need to be there this Sunday. Will you?

Life is just beginning. Hallelujah!—translation: Praise the Lord!

### FURTHER STUDY

Some may yet need more time and study. If so, the following "Two Ways to Live" explains how the Gospel of God's grace is laid out in the Bible. Sharpen your pencil, take your Bible in hand, and dig in. It's only your soul that is at stake.

### TWO WAYS TO LIVE: A BRIEF LOOK AT THE MESSAGE OF CHRISTIANITY

What is Christianity about? What does it mean to be a Christian? Most people have their own ideas about these questions, but in the end, God's ideas are the important ones. What does He say being a Christian is really about? That's what we'll be looking at in this short study: God's definition of Christianity as He spells it out in the Bible. There are six basic points.

## 1. God—The Loving Creator and Ruler

God is the loving ruler of the world. He made it, and He made us to rule and care for the world—under His authority.

Find Revelation 4:11 in a Bible (Revelation is near the back). Read it and then try to write answers to the following questions from what you've read.

a. Why should we honor and praise God?

b. Is there anything in creation that does not depend on God's will? Explain.

c. What attitude should we have to a God like this?

## 2. Humanity in Rebellion

When we look at the world, however, we can see that things are not the way they should be. This is because we reject God as our ruler by trying to run our lives without Him. Have we done a good job of running ourselves, our society, and our world? Support your answer with examples.

Now read Romans 3:10–13 from the Bible.

a. According to this passage, how many righteous people are there?

b. How many people really seek God?

c. How many people have turned away from God's loving rule?

Note this carefully: Some people rebel quietly by just ignoring God. Others rebel more visibly by doing things that everyone recognizes as sinful. But either way, it's rebellion against God. The real question is: What will God do about it? Let's find out.

### 3. God Won't Let People Keep on Rebelling Forever

God cares enough about us to take our rebellion seriously and to call us to account.
Read Hebrews 9:27.

   a.  What does the future hold for everyone?

   b.  What must everyone face after death?

God's punishment for rebellion is death and judgment. This might sound hard, and many people don't like to believe that God could feel so strongly about our rebellion. But justice isn't justice unless it brings sin to account. It's simply wrong to turn a blind eye.

The bad news is very bad, but the good news is wonderful. God has provided a remedy for the disastrous position in which we find ourselves.

### 4. Jesus—The Man Who Dies for Rebels

God loved the world so much that He sent His Son into the world—Jesus Christ. Jesus obeyed God completely. He was the one person who deserved no punishment. He lived a wonderful life of selfless giving, truth, and integrity, but He was executed as a common criminal. By dying on the cross, He, the perfect man, took our punishment and brought us free forgiveness.
Read 1 Peter 3:18.

   a.  Why did Christ die?

   b.  Who is the righteous person mentioned here? Who are the unrighteous?

c. Which of the two terms describes you?

d. What can Christ's death do for you?

The death of Jesus is not the end of the story. Before He died, Jesus said He would come back from the grave after three days. At the time nobody believe Him. But then . . .

## 5. Jesus—The Risen Ruler

God accepted Jesus' death as payment in full for our sins and raised Him from the dead. The risen Jesus is now what humanity was always meant to be: God's ruler of the world. Jesus has conquered death and now gives new life to us. One day He will return to judge the world. Read Philippians 2:9–11.

a. What place has God given to Jesus?

b. What attitude should we have toward Jesus?

c. Whether by choice or otherwise, who will eventually bow down to the authority of Jesus?

By rising from the dead, Jesus proved once and for all that He did indeed have all the power and authority He claimed to have as the Son of God. That leaves us with only two options . . .

## 6. The Two Ways to Live

*Our Way*

• Reject God as ruler
• Try to run our own lives our own way

Result   • Condemned by God
        • Facing death and judgment

*God's New Way*

- Submit to Jesus as Lord
- Rely on Jesus' death and resurrection

Result    • Forgiven by God
          • Given eternal life

Read John 3:36.

a.  What two types of people are described here?

b.  What must you do to have eternal life?

c.  Why would God's anger (wrath) remain on certain people?

d.  Which of these two options is the way you want to live?

## What Should I Do Next?

You may want to think more about the truths covered in this brief study. You can get to know Jesus better by reading Mark's gospel.

If, however, you know that you're ready to give your life to God by submitting to Jesus' rule, you should pray a simple prayer in your own words. Ask God to forgive you for ignoring Him and rebelling. Ask Him to help you let Jesus run your life and to rely on His death for forgiveness and eternal life.

From that point on, it's a matter of living out your new way of life day by day—but you won't be on your own. God will be with you all the way. He'll keep speaking to you (as you read the Bible); He'll keep listening to you and helping you (as you pray to Him); He'll help you to change and live His way (by His Spirit who lives within you); and He'll provide brothers and sisters to encourage you along the way (as you meet with other Christians).

Moody Press, a ministry of Moody Bible Institute,
is designed for education, evangelization, and edification.
If we may assist you in knowing more about Christ
and the Christian life, please write us without obligation:
Moody Press, c/o MLM, Chicago, IL 60610.